The 13 Judges

by

A.M.S. Gooding

DECEMBER 1986
Published by
GOSPEL TRACT PUBLICATIONS
48 York Street, Glasgow, Scotland G2 8JW

ISBN 0 948417 10 2

Typeset, Printed and Bound by
GOSPEL TRACT PUBLICATIONS
48 York Street, Glasgow G2 8JW

Contents

Introduction

THIRTEEN JUDGES: their history makes up the major part of the Book of Judges. There were fifteen judges altogether, Eli and Samuel having their place in the first book of Samuel. This volume will concern itself only with the thirteen whose lives are recorded in the book where "there was no king in Israel and every man did that which was right in his own eyes." Thirteen is a strange number; its first mention in the word of God is in Genesis 14:4: "Twelve years they served Chedorlaomer, and in the thirteenth year they rebelled." So according to the law of first mention, thirteen is associated with rebellion and this is its characteristic feature throughout the word of God.

The context of this book will help us in its application for teaching in these days. The book follows the record of Moses and Joshua, and is followed by the record of the lives of Saul, David and Solomon. Moses is undoubtedly a picture of the Lord Jesus, as Redeemer of His people, and God also promised to raise up unto Israel, "from amongst thy brethren," a prophet like unto Moses. Ere Moses goes to the top of the mount, at the command of God, he appointed Joshua to be his successor, to fulfil all that the Lord commanded Moses. Joshua was leader by divine appointment. He is an apt picture of the Holy Spirit of God, the Vicar of Christ, sent to continue the things Jesus had begun to do and teach until the day He was taken up. After that, Peter declared, "He being by the right hand of God exalted, and having received of the Father the promise of the Holy Ghost hath poured

forth that which ye now see and hear." Joshua led the
people into the land in association with the leaders of the
twelve tribes, and can we suggest that in a similar way
the Holy Spirit of God led God's people into the age in
which we live in association with the twelve.

The Book of Judges records for us the lives of thirteen
men, raised up to be judges, not in the days of Joshua,
nor in the days of the elders that outlived Joshua, but
from the days of another generation which knew not the
Lord nor yet the works which He had done for Israel.

Examining these details one concludes that the best
way to look at the lives of these judges for our spiritual
good is to recognise that they belonged to the period that
commenced about two generations after Joshua; and
thus the truth connected with them will be best applied
in the period commencing about two generations after
the descent of the Spirit of God and the commencement
of the church period, in other words, the post-apostolic
period; similar to that brought before us in Revelation 2
and 3 in the letters to the seven churches of Asia.

After the Book of Judges, I repeat, there are the
biographies of Saul, David and Solomon. Saul, the man
of the flesh, the enemy of David, is removed in order that
the warrior king David might establish the kingdom,
and Solomon might sit upon the throne as the king of
prosperity and peace. These three thus form a faint
picture of events to take place after the church has been
taken home.

I suggest therefore that the book is applicable in
teaching to the period from post-apostolic days until the
rapture of the church.

It is interesting that Joshua did not appoint these
men; that they did not appoint each other, or succeed

each other in a certain family. They were raised up from different backgrounds, individually by God Himself. We no doubt realise that in the age in which we are living there are those who lead God's people who were not appointed by the Lord Jesus on earth nor by revelation from heaven, nor are they appointed by men, nor by natural succession; but by way of contrast the New Testament says on certain men, "Take heed unto yourselves, and to all the flock, in the which the Holy Ghost hath made you overseers to feed the church of God, which He hath purchased with His own blood." We shall then look at the judges in two ways: first, as pictures of New Testament overseers, elders or bishops; and secondly, as examples of different types of believers who make up the one flock of this dispensation.

We must draw attention to the fact that the judges were all from differing backgrounds — different tribes, different vocations, different social classes, having differing educational qualifications, some wealthy, some poor — but they should all be raised up the Holy Spirit of God. These men came from different tribes: Judah, Benjamin, Manasseh, Gilead, Dan, Levi. They were from different backgrounds: a soldier, a diplomat, a farmer, a brigand, a priest. Some seemed to be great and renowned and rich, others were insignificant and poor. One amongst these thirteen was a woman.

What wondrous lessons the Spirit of God would teach us — let us go prayerfully through the book with Him.

Othniel — The Ideal Judge

The first three enemies that God allows to challenge the Israelites and bring them into subjection are presented to us in the opening chapters of the Book of Judges. The first is Chushan-rishathaim, the meaning of whose name we shall see is "the blackness of double wickedness", apt picture of the world. The second is Eglon, the King of Moab, who represents "the ugliness of the flesh". Thirdly, Jabin, the king whose place is on the mounds, and who has lesser kings under him. He represents the prince of the power of the air, the spirit that now worketh in the sons of disobedience. He has 'lesser kings' under him, called in the Ephesian epistle "principalities, powers, rulers of the darkness of this world, spiritual wickedness in high places." These three enemies, (1) the world (2) the flesh (3) the devil, are the three opposing forces that God's people have to meet and against which they must fight if they are going to possess their possessions and live triumphantly for God.

"And the children of Israel dwelt among the Canaanites, Hittites, Amorites, Perizzites, Hivites and Jebusites: and they took their daughters to be their wives, and gave their daughters to their sons, and served their gods. And the children of Israel did evil in the sight of the Lord, and forgot the Lord their God, and served Baalim and the groves" (Judges 3:5-7). A better translation would be: "and served Baalim and Ashtaroth." It isn't that they served the grove of trees; the idea of the grove is that it was a place of worship, but the worship was of Ashtaroth. One of the names given to the feminine deity, the wife or the consort of Baal, she is called in the Old Testament scriptures "the Queen of Heaven". You'll remember that they made cakes to the Queen of Heaven in an idolatrous situation. "Therefore the anger of the Lord was hot against Israel, and he sold them into the hand of Chushan-rishathaim eight years. And when the children of Israel cried unto the Lord, the Lord raised up a deliverer [R.V. a saviour] to the children of Israel, who delivered them, even Othniel the son of Kenaz, Caleb's younger brother. And the Spirit of the Lord came upon him, and he judged Israel, and went out to war: and the Lord delivered Chushan-rishathaim king of Mesopotamia into his hand; and his hand prevailed against Chushan-rishathaim. And the land had rest forty years. And Othniel the son of Kenaz died."

Having failed to destroy the people of the land, they allowed them to live among them. They took their daughters to be their wives, and gave their daughters to their sons, and as a result they served their gods. A simple lesson that the saints of God really need to learn. If you and I sit down in companionship with the people of the world, the result will be that our affections will be entwined around them. Not a spiritual affection, but a natural affection. And the natural result of people living in close proximity is that they fall in love with each other, and marriage is the result.

Of course, these people knew perfectly well that God would have His people to dwell alone — He had told them that. Balaam had even declared from the top of the mountain that God's people must dwell alone. But disregarding what God had said, they arrive in the land, live among the people of the land, admire the daughters of the land, love them, and marry them. The sons and the daughters of God's people marrying the ungodly! The next step is very easy: if you live with a man who is an idolater, or with a woman who is an idolater, and they fill their homes and their lives with idolatrous things, the result will be — "they served their gods." It's an old thing, it has happened so many times. It begins with eating and drinking together, then marrying, then worshipping together. You remember that when Baalam could not judge God's people, "he taught Balak to cast a stumbling block before the children of Israel." The secret of success against Israel was not to curse from without but to corrupt from within. Doubtless Baalam taught Balak to send out the daughters of Moab and they ate and drank, then they committed fornication, and they served their gods. Twenty-four thousand of them fell beneath the disciplining hand of God. So simple, isn't it? Eat and drink together, then marry together, then you're right on the road to idolatry.

1st Corinthians 10 is a very interesting chapter — it's all about eating and drinking. It teaches that eating and drinking always has certain associations. It says, "Our fathers were all baptized unto Moses in the cloud and in the sea, and did all eat the same spiritual meat, and did all drink the same spiritual drink: for they drank of that spiritual Rock that followed them: and that Rock was Christ." Paul teaches that people who eat and drink that kind of spiritual food are expected to live a certain way. But he says, "With many of them God was not well pleased." Why? Read the next twelve verses and look up the references in the Old Testament scriptures — it's all about eating and drinking and the conduct associated therewith.

They despised the manna, and the judgment of God came upon them. They made a golden calf, and the Word says, "The people sat down to eat and drink, and they rose up to play." And they were on the road to idolatry. The next incident is with regard to the daughters of Moab: they ate, they drank, they committed fornication. They were on the road to idolatry. From 1 Corinthians 10 we see that there were two places where men and women ate. There was the table of demons in the idols' temple. There was also the Lord's table connected with the bread and cup used for the Lord's Supper. People who sat down at the table of demons lived lives of fornication and idolatry. People who sat down at the Lord's table lived lives of holiness and divine worship. Eating and drinking leads to a certain path and has certain consequences. So when people live together and eat and drink together, their sons and daughters marry, and departure from the Lord follows. Of course, these parents were to blame — these parents who settled down among the ungodly, and the ungodly were allowed to settle down among them. "They took their daughters to be their wives and gave their daughters to their sons." So I read of two generations here. The generation who chose to go and live among the ungodly — what did they do? They took the daughters of the ungodly to be their wives and gave their daughters to their sons. They married the ungodly too. Were not the parents to blame?

That teaches a very serious lesson. My dear Christian parent, do you eat and drink with the ungodly? I am not saying you should refrain from eating a meal with unsaved persons. What I mean is, do you have worldly social contacts? do you make your round of socialising amongst the ungodly? and are you perfectly at home sitting at their table? and will you invite them to your table, and so compromise on divine things that they might feel at home in your home? And so they and you, and your daughters and your sons, and their daughters and their sons, are perfectly socially happy together. Where does it lead to? Well! eating together leads to marrying together, and this takes the hearts of God's people away from the Lord, away to the things of the world and the things that are contrary to God. It's a very simple lesson. Sometimes parents are to blame when their children marry the ungodly.

I have known dear Christians who have moved from certain parts of the town or city because the people in the other parts are a little higher up the social ladder. Sometimes their sons and their daughters marry folks in that locality as a result. I have seen Christian parents take their children away from an ordinary Sunday school in an ordinary Gospel Hall and send them to some other religious organization. Why? It's further up the social scale, you know, and there are people who are our class, or better class, that our young folks will meet there. And of course they do meet there, and they marry folks that are often higher socially — but not saved. Who is to blame? The social climbers! The social climbers among the people of God that want to go up the social ladder, and to get there will take their wives and families into circumstances where, for natural advantage, they will eat and drink and be at home with the ungodly. Then they sit and weep when their young folks marry non-Christian partners and go into the world.

What did God do? It says, "The children of Israel did evil in the sight of the Lord" (you know what they had done — they had married the ungodly), "and forgot the Lord their God, and served Baalim" (that is the automatic result), "and the anger of the Lord was hot against Israel, and he sold them." Not that He gained anything by selling them. He didn't sell them for money in order to become enriched, but He sold them like slaves into bondage. Who did it? You say, the devil? My Bible doesn't say so. My Bible says God did. He sold His people into the enemy hands — yes. Why did He do it? He did it because He was going to discipline His people. Here's a lesson we must learn. We are so apt in the days in which we live, when trial comes into the lives of God's people, to say, "It's just one of those things," there's no real cause for it, it just happens to me the way it happens to thousands of other folk.

In the Hebrew epistle we learn that when trial and difficulty come into the lives of God's people, we haven't just to shrug our shoulders and say, "It's just one of those things." We have neither to despise chastening nor faint under it. Nevertheless "it yieldeth the peaceable fruits of righteousness to them that are exercised thereby." Please do not misunderstand me. One would not suggest that every bit of trial or sickness in the lives of God's people is because of unconfessed, unforgiven sin. It certainly is not. But every bit of sickness and trial that does come into our lives should make us say, "Why? why has this come upon me? why am I passing through this experience?" It may be you are passing through this experience for the education of some other Christian. It may be you pass through a certain experience in order that in the trial you may exhibit the very graces of Christ, and God will be glorified by the quiet submissive way you endure the trial. Or it may be you pass through the trial because God wants to bring you nearer to Him than you are now. But, on the other hand, it may be the hand of divine discipline. God may be wanting you to listen and to respond. And when He acts in that way, the Old Testament uses the term: "God's anger was hot against his people Israel, and he sold them." That is, God in a paternal way may be grieved with our behaviour, and in paternal anger He may lift a Father's hand, and discipline us for our good and for our restoration, that we might be "partakers of His holiness".

Let us consider what this discipline was. Of what had they been guilty? They had been guilty of living among the world, marrying worldlings, of worshipping the world's gods. First of all they had been shaking hands with the world, living in among them. Then they were attracted by a worldly face and figure, the young man would do all he could to please the worldly girl, and then he would marry her. And into a new home that worldly girl brings worldly things until those worldly things fill the heart of the young man who knows God, and the home becomes more worldly, until the gods of the world are there. Is that not right? Is that not the way it works? You marry someone that's not saved and soon you'll have to try to accommodate worldly fancies, and you will soon have to allow into your home worldly things. And will you not very soon find that your heart develops an appetite for worldly things, and the things of God will get less and less place, until God is out, the reading of the Scriptures gone? The things of the world will take the place of Christ. When this becomes the experience of God's people, how will God discipline them?

Notice what it says: "Therefore the anger of the Lord

was hot against Israel, and he sold them into the hand of Chushan-rishathaim, king of Mesopotamia," or king of Aram. It's the place from which Abram was called. The place where he heard the God of glory say, "Get out from thy kindred and from thy father's house unto a land that I will show thee."

What kind of world was he saved from? Let us each ask a further question: "What kind of world were we saved from? Has it a king, and what is his name?" *Chushan* means "blackness". Remember Abram's three sons: one was Ham; his eldest son was Cush, meaning black. Then there is the second part of his name, *Rishathaim,* which means "double wickedness". So this man is the king of Mesopotamia, and he is called "the blackness of double wickedness". In the epistle to the Colossians, chapter 1, we read, "Who hath delivered us out of the kingdom of darkness and hath translated us into the kingdom of the Son of his love." So there is the kingdom of darkness in contradistinction to the "kingdom of the Son of his love." We are now the children of light, but we once belonged to the kingdom of darkness. The kingdom of darkness is that world to which we once belonged. Abram once belonged to Aram, which was now ruled over by "the blackness of double wickedness". So we ourselves once belonged to that old world which is the kingdom of darkness, ruled by the god of this world, Satan himself.

Because God was angry with His people He disciplined them. How did He do it? Notice what He did not do. He did not say, "I am going to send you back to the place from which Abram came. You are no longer fit to live in this land. Go back to Ur of the Chaldees." Oh no! He didn't send them back to where they originally belonged: He left them in the land, but He brought the king of the land from which Abram was delivered to dominate them in the land to which they had come. He didn't send them back to Ur of the Chaldees, but He sent the king from Ur of the Chaldees into the land. And that King from Aram — from Mesopotamia — he crossed the border, he came into the land, he dominated God's people in the land and brought them into bondage.

What is God teaching us? Just this! My dear fellow Christian, if you have links with the world that fill your life with worldliness, and fill your heart with worldliness, and fill your home with worldliness, God will not cut you off. You're saved. You're saved for Heaven. God will not send you back to the world and say, "You're not fit to be my people." What will He do? Listen! If you allow the world to come into your life and into your home and give it a place it should not have in your affections: that world from which you have been saved will cross the border of the place where you now are, and will bring you into bondage there. Once it dominated you in the land of darkness before you were saved. If, as a Christian, you eat with the world, link with the world, marry the world, worship the world's things: God may allow that world, that system of the blackness of double darkness, to triumph against you, to come into your home, your heart, your life, until the world from which you were saved, will again become your master. So while it's true you have been saved from the world and saved for Heaven, yet when God's people become worldly He allows the world to take them into bondage until they cry out for God to deliver them from the world.

In these verses, first of all they wanted the world, they wanted to be friendly with the world, they wanted to marry the world, wanted to worship with the world. Says God, You want the world — I'll bring it to your very doorstep. I'll bring the blackness of double wickedness to your very home and you'll groan under the burden of the king of the world until you cry, "Oh, Lord! deliver me from worldliness."

My dear brother, my dear sister, possibly there was a day when you were first married when on your knees together you thanked God for His goodness to you. There wasn't a bit of carpet on the floor, there was very little furniture. You knew that God was leading you, you knew you were married in the Lord, and what little you had it was all for God, and Christ was the very centre of your home. There was no worldliness about your living, then. The years have gone by, and God has been good to you. More of the comforts of God's goodness have come into your life year by year. But along with that, gradually, a little socialising with the world. A little of letting the world into your home. And the more of the world, the less of the Word of God. Until the family altar dropped out, and prayer together dropped out. And that time of reading the Scriptures alone — that dropped out. And in its place, one after another, the things of the world have come in. Until — if you're honest in the presence of God — you know the trouble in your life is worldliness. My very dear friends, is that what it is like in your home or my home? Look back on your life: there was a time in your life when God first saved you, maybe before you were married, when Christ was everything in your life, so much so, that you may think some of the things you did then were ridiculously extreme. You acted that way because you loved the Lord. As the years have gone by your conscience has become dulled, more of the world has come in, and there has been more and more compromise, until that once-delicate conscience of yours has become almost seared with a hot iron. And you've got the world in your heart, in your thinking, in your ambitions.

Let me say again, there was a day when the Lord put into your hands children to rear for Himself, and you sheltered them from the world then. But as the years went by, in order that they might not be oddities in the eyes of the world, and to give them credibility in worldly circles, there was more and more compromise. Till, maybe, you think on your family and their prosperity, how they have got on; but the bitterness of it all is this: they've gone into the world. When we allow the world into our individual lives and into our united lives as husband and wife and into our family lives, God disciplines us by allowing the worldliness of the kingdom from which we were delivered to enslave us where we are — the kingdom of the blackness of double wickedness! I mean, there can come a time in the lives of God's people, in the life of an individual who has been living for God, when he allows the world to come in —only a little. And then a little bit more of the world —not intending to become worldly. But the time comes when God allows the discipline of the kingdom of double wickedness to come in, and God says, "You want the world — here it is." And the man or woman who once walked with God, who played with the world, suddenly finds themselves in the grip of the world and can't get out. It's the discipline of God. If we hug the world to our breasts, God will allow the world to hug us. If we play with the thing we call the world, God will allow the world to swallow us. He will do it just by giving us what we want. Awful discipline, isn't it?

Is there a brother or sister reading this book who, after their partner sleeps at night, sits alone and longs for the days of godliness you once knew, longs for the lack of worldliness you once knew? Is there a husband or wife reading this, and you find it very difficult to be honest with each other and say, "Look here, dear, we've missed it. We've got all these things, but we've let the world in and we've lost the presence of Christ." Is there anyone honest enough in the presence of God, when they look at the family gone into the world, to get into God's presence, with tears, and acknowledge that you let the world in and the result is catastrophic?

You see, God brought His people to this point when they were under the domination of Chushan-rishathaim for eight long years. Eight, of course, is the number of new creation. It's the number of new beginning. And having groaned under the burden of the world from which Abram had been delivered, they cried unto the Lord to be delivered. What a day it would be in our lives, wouldn't it, if God's people cried to be delivered from worldliness. Cried that the world would be pushed again from the throne of their hearts, and their lives, and their homes — to be as free of the world as God intended us to be when the New Testament says, "By whom the world is crucified unto me, and I unto the world."

Do we not, every one of us in the presence of God, find a need in our souls to be delivered from worldliness? None of us in the assembly are as godly as we ought to be, none of us as separate as we ought to be. Every one of

us possibly looking back and realising that the world has
made incursions into our lives that never should have
been. If God would bring us to where He brought these
people — "they cried unto the Lord"! That would be a
great day in New Testament churches: when we begin
to cry unto the Lord to deliver us from our worldliness,
to bring us again to realise that the cross lies between us
and the world.

When God's people get there, this chapter says, "The
Lord raised up a saviour." That's lovely, isn't it? My
dear brother, do you want to be saved from the world?
My dear sister, do you want to be saved from the world?
I'm not talking about your eternal salvation, I'm talking
about worldliness. God raises up a saviour. In these
judges I see a picture of the Lord Jesus. But as we go
through Judges we are going to see these judges as
pictures of overseeing brethren in the present day. And
my dear fellow-elders, I want to talk to you, as I talk to
myself. Are you a saviour from worldliness? God's
people need saviours, they need deliverers, they need
leaders. Saviours, deliverers, leaders — from worldliness.

Whom did God raise up? Othniel. Othniel has a most
interesting history. You find that Othniel is the son of
Kenaz, i.e., of the family of Kenaz. If you go back into
the Book of Genesis you find that this was the name of a
relative of Esau. Had these relatives of Esau married
into a family of Judah, and so belonged to the tribe of
Judah? I think that's an apt picture of you and I, isn't it?
Have you not, my dear brother, got a connection with
Esau? And yet you belong to the tribe of Judah — the
tribe of praise, singing songs of praise to God. And so
here is Caleb, first of all, and Othniel who was related to
him: they belonged to Kenaz. They have Esau

connections — the man of the flesh — but through God's grace they were brought into the tribe of Judah and given a song of praise. Everyone has Esau connections — the old flesh. Through sovereign grace we have been brought to know Christ as our Saviour, and we sing songs of praise because of deliverance.

Let us look at Othniel in chapter 1, verse 10. He is associated with Hebron. Hebron is the place of fellowship, it's the place of communion, it's the place of being in contact with God. My dear fellow-elder, do you know anything about fellowship with God? know anything about communion? know anything about oneness with God? Abram, you will remember, was a great deliverer: he brought Lot out of Sodom, delivering him from the battle of the kings. Where had he been? Hebron — the place of fellowship. My dear fellow-elder, do you know anything about fellowship? I'm not talking about being in fellowship in the local assembly. You couldn't be an elder in the local assembly without being in fellowship in that sense. Do you know anything about communion with God? know anything about oneness with God? Do you get right deep into God's presence? Are you communing with God during the hours of the day? Are you a man of Hebron? To be an effectual overseer in the assembly of God's people you must know what it is to abide in God, to abide in Christ. You must know fellowship with God, you must have a sanctuary life, you must be at home in His presence. My dear brother, you'll never lead God's people from worldliness unless you start there. It's only a man of the sanctuary that values divine things. Abram valued those. What did Lot value? The cities of the plain with its subsequent judgment.

Dear elders, do you live in Hebron? And as you come to God's people, meet them in the assembly and in the street, do you come as men who know the fellowship with God?

I find now a third thing about him. He was a man who was challenged to take a city, and he took a city because he loved a girl called Achsah. So through pure and true love he took a city. (Judges 1:10-15.) I'm not asking you if you have a true love to your wife, but have you a true love for Christ? — an essential qualification for every overseer. The last chapter of John's Gospel says, "Simon Peter, lovest thou me?" — feed my sheep, feed my lambs. That was the necessary requirement — lovest thou Me? Nobody should ever be persuaded to be an overseer, pushed to be an overseer, constrained to be an overseer. No, the man who is a real overseer, he's doing it out of real love. And the primary thing is not love to the saints, the primary thing is love to the Lord. "Lovest thou me?" — then feed My sheep.

My dear brother, are you an overseer because you like the office? because you like the name? because you have ability to organise? Or do you really love the Lord? Recognise the members of the assembly as being the Lord's sheep, and you'll look after the sheep for Him. You'll not be so ready to let them go if you realise they are His sheep. You'll be very tender with them if you realise what He paid for them. Every sheep is valuable.

I find something else — that because of his love he smote a city called Kirjath-sepher, and then he changed the name of the city into Debir. Kirjath-sepher means "the city of the book". Then its name was changed to be "the word of God". All overseers must be men who take the City of the Book. My dear brother, when you have taken the city of the book, that book must be to you the Word of God. Come now! have you taken the city of the book? have you taken the book? All New Testament overseers must be apt to teach. We have said often that does not mean you have to be gifted as a teacher to occupy the platform. But you must take the book. You must know the book. How can you lead God's people aright if you don't know? How can you deliver them from worldliness if you don't know the book? Every overseer must know the book.

Young people, how are you progressing with getting to know the book? How many hours a day do you spend on the book? How diligently do you study the book? Are you able to handle it, understand it, give a right exegesis of it, know what it means in its context? So that when the saints of God come to you in a coming day and say, "I've got a problem here: can you guide me from God's Word?" — you know the book. Worldly wisdom won't do. Saying, "What we have always done" — that won't do. Saying, "Our fathers did it this way or that way" —that won't do. They say in Christendom, We've always done it this way. You must know the book, and be able to prove from it what is right. Othniel took the city of the book. Come, young men, you wouldn't find fault with me if I said that what is wrong today is that there is a dearth of men who have taken the book. Take the book, spend time on it, work on it, sacrifice to get at it, get to know the book. When you can expound in its context what this book means — that's essential, but not all that is essential. When you've taken this book so that you can give the sense and meaning of the passages, there must be something more. This book must be to you the Word of God. You could get to know this book like a treatise in algebra, or get to know this book like the latest book on mathematics. But this book is more. It is the Word of God for your soul. It's God speaking. Before its pages you must tremble. God is near to the man that trembleth at His Word. My brethren, is that what the book is to you? Is that what the book is to me? It's only men like that that can deliver God's people from worldliness.

Another thing about this man — he had an equal yoke. He not only married a woman who belonged to Israel, but a woman who had spiritual desires, who said to her husband, "Ask for me"— she encouraged her husband to pray. And not only that, but when she met her father she said, "You have given me the south country; give me also springs of water." My dear brother, what kind of wife have you? What kind of girl are you going to marry? You cannot read the New Testament scriptures through and come to the subject of overseers without finding their wives mentioned. My dear brother, tell me, did you marry a Christian? More, did you marry a godly Christian? Did you marry a girl who encouraged you to pray? And did you marry a girl who was already in enjoyment of the south country but who wanted more — wanted springs of water? Did you? If there is a man like that, he is a happy man and has one of the essential qualifications to be an overseer. If a man hasn't got that, he has a big drawback in his life when it comes to shepherding God's assembly.

That's the kind of man I find in chapter 3 whom God raised up to deliver His people. Where are the Othniels today? For the Othniels, by character, are the men God will raise up in these days to deliver His people from worldliness. Qualification number one was this: he hadn't done what the people had done. They had gone and married the sons and daughters of the land, and that was the beginning of their worldliness. He had married in the Lord, he had married for God. He and his wife were going the right road. This man — a man who knew the Word of God — was able to lead God's people. He had taken the book. It was really to him the Word of God.

As you meditate on these things, I want you to link Othniel and this chapter with the first epistle of John chapter 2 verses 14 to 17. There you will find New Testament spiritual Othniels. It says, "I write unto you, young men." That's Othniel, isn't it? His name means 'lion of God' — strong man for God. "Because ye are strong." How were the young men strong? Because "the Word of God abideth in you." Is that not Othniel? He took the city of the book — the Word of God. It was abiding in him. It doesn't mean young men physically, it is those who have taken the Book as the Word of God. Has it made us strong and helped us to win battles in overcoming the Wicked One? Othniel was like that. It's men like that that God raises up to deliver His people from the world. John in his epistle is still addressing young men when he says, "Love not the world, neither the things that are in the world. If any man love the world, the love of the Father is not in him. For all that is in the world, the lust of the flesh, and the lust of the eyes, and the pride of life, is not of the Father, but is of the world. And the world passeth away, and the lust thereof: but he that doeth the will of God abideth for ever." So it is this kind of Othniel who is told, "Love not the world." This Othniel will stand as a spiritual young man among God's people, and be a saviour. And it is young men and older men who have become strong because of the Word of God that abideth in them, who have overcome the wicked one, have said "no" to the world: these are the men God will raise up to deliver His people from worldliness.

But let me talk to the other saints, including the elders. Only a few are elders, but all are God's people in danger of worldliness, and our need to conquer the world is the same. What is it? Spend time in Hebron. Reassess our love for the Lord. Get to know the Book. Tremble before it as the Word of God. Then in the power of instruction from this Book, like Othniel, filled with the Spirit of God, let us cast out worldliness from our own hearts, from our family relationships, from our associations. After Othniel had delivered God's people from their worldliness, the land had peace for forty years until Othniel died. When God's people in our day are delivered from their worldliness, then the assemblies will have peace, prosperity, and divine blessing. The presence of God shall be known by us as we've never known it before, and Christ shall become everything in our lives.

Ehud — The Diplomat

"The children of Israel did evil in the sight of the Lord" is followed now with "And the children of Israel did evil again in the sight of the Lord." It is found again and again in this book (3:7; 3:12; 4:1; 6:1; 10:6; 13:1). The record of departure and recovery in the days when there was no king in Israel and every man did that which was right in his own eyes.

God allows another enemy to come in for the discipline of His people: "He strengthened Eglon the King of Moab against Israel." Let us discover what the Word of God has to say about Moab. His beginning is found in Genesis 19 when Lot, having been delivered from Sodom and its judgment as a result of God remembering Abraham, makes his way first of all to Zoar, and then because he feared to dwell in Zoar he dwelt in a cave with his two daughters. As a result of the sinfulness of those two daughters, two boys were born to be a perpetual shame to Lot. The firstborn daughter was the instigator of the vile plan, and to her there was born a boy. And we read, "The firstborn bare a son and called his name Moab: the same is the father of the Moabites unto this day" (Genesis 19:37). Moab commenced its existence in the foul gutter of gross sin — unmentionable sin. Isaiah tells us a little of the end of Moab: "In that day Moab shall be trodden down ... even as straw is trodden down in the water of the dunghill" (25:10 R.V.) Thus we learn that Moab from the beginning to the end is associated with a cesspool of immorality.

27

Notice also that Moab was a close relative of Abraham's, a half-cousin to Isaac, near of kin: and we are thereby taught that this evil thing pictured in Moab, called "the flesh", the old nature, is still present in every believer. It is not eradicated. So that John can write, "If we say that we have no sin [the thing, the root], we deceive ourselves, and the truth is not in us." Have we not all learned by bitter experience that this is very true?

Associated also with Moab are two other features, namely ease and pride: "Moab hath been at ease from his youth, he hath settled on his lees, he hath not been emptied from one vessel to another" (Jeremiah 48:11). He was perfectly at home in his original location, content where he was. He equates spiritually with the expression in the Revelation: "those that dwell on the earth." Earth dwellers — no horizon beyond this scene! Again, "We have heard of the pride of Moab, he is very proud, even of his haughtiness, and his wrath, his boastings" etc. (Isaiah 16:6).

We conclude that Moab represents that thing within us — the flesh — that is morally base, is the seat of such works as "adultery, fornication, uncleanness, lasciviousness, idolatry, witchcraft, hatred, variance, emulations, wrath, strife, seditions, heresies, envying, murders, drunkenness, revellings and such like" (Galatians 5:19-21). This is Moab, and he dwells within each one of us.

With Moab are gathered the children of Ammon and Amalek (Judges 3:13). Ammon descended from the sinful association between Lot and his younger daughter, so that he had a corrupt beginning. His history is also associated with bestial cruelty: "because they ripped up the women with child of Gilead, that they might enlarge their border" (Amos 1:13).

Amalek has also an interesting history. He is first mentioned in Genesis 36:12. Verse 10 says, "These are the names of Esau's sons: Eliphaz, the son of Adah the wife of Esau ..." Verse 11 adds, "And the sons of Eliphaz were Teman, Omar, Zepho, Gatam and Kenaz." (These were all legitimately born) but now the Spirit of God adds, "And Timna was concubine to Eliphaz, Esau's son; and she bare to Eliphaz Amalek" (verse 12). Esau, of course, represents that which has natural priority, for Esau was born first. But the principle applies: "The first man is of the earth, earthy" (1 Cor. 15:47). "That which is born of the flesh is flesh, and that which is born of the Spirit is spirit" (John 3:9). Esau reminds us of the old nature, those old habits, old tendencies — the flesh in contrast to the Spirit. However, consider that while descending from Esau, Amalek was conceived out of wedlock and therefore would bring before us *the old nature degenerated*. One should remember there is good flesh and bad flesh (see Philippians 3:4, good flesh; 3:18, bad flesh) but both are flesh and therefore unacceptable to God. There is good flesh as illustrated in King Saul, and bad ugly flesh pictured in Eglon.

These three principles work together in our beings —all base desires of the flesh to bring us into bondage.

"The Lord strengthened Eglon the king of Moab against Israel." This was a discipline of God. What a warning is this! Many a person has been deceived into believing that they could play with sin, that they could pander to the desires of the flesh like playing with a toy: only to find, flesh is strengthened against them, and a seeming toy becomes an iron chain. Fellow Christian, you and I cannot afford to play with sin or accommodate its desires — should we do so it will eventually bind us and ruin our usefulness for God. Did not Paul guided by the Spirit write, "But I buffet my body, and bring it into subjection, lest that by any means when I had preached to others, I myself should be rejected [or disapproved]" (1 Cor. 9:27)? As God allowed worldliness to enslave the worldly (see previous chapter) so here He allows the flesh to be strengthened against those who indulge the flesh.

Certain features recorded about Eglon, King of Moab, help us to develop the picture.

(1) *He was a very fat man* (v. 17). (His army was composed of very fat men, v. 29). This man was so fat that he was ugly, fat bulged out everywhere. Nothing attractive, nothing admirable. A true picture of flesh with all its awful works manifested.

(2) *He sat alone in his cooling house* (v. 20). Flesh manifesting itself in all its ugliness does not make for good companionship. But more: flesh becomes inflamed with passion. Thus Paul writes, "It is better to marry than to burn" (1 Corinthians 7:9). It needs a cooling house (summer parlour).

(3) *He was seated and pampered* (v. 20). Thus flesh loves rest, ease, idleness, time to satisfy all its desires.

(4) *When slain "the dirt came out"* (v. 22), for flesh is corruption within. Even whited sepulchres had dead men's bones within, and "out of the heart of man proceed evil thoughts, adulteries, fornications, murders, thefts, covetousness, wickedness, deceit, lasciviousness, an evil eye, railing, pride, foolishness; all these evil things come from within" (Mark 7:21-23).

This is the enemy. And from such an enemy God's people needed a saviour.

When Eglon was strengthened against God's people, he, together with Ammon and Amalek, possessed the city of palm trees. This city is of course Jericho, and you remember that Jericho was their first triumph in the land; for God's complete deliverance was to bring them out, to bring them through, and to bring them in. Once they had crossed the Jordan their first triumph in the land was to take the city of palm trees. But now the flesh was strengthened against them: Eglon's army had crossed the border. And the first thing Eglon robbed them of, and possessed, was the seat of their earliest triumph. I wonder if that will strike a chord in the hearts of any of the dear saints of God. You go back to the moment when, having trusted Christ as Saviour, and having the full assurance of God's salvation, you knew something of your first triumph, shall we say, in the land of your salvation. What a victory it was when there was some old habit of the flesh which you abandoned! Something in which you had indulged for many years. It was a master in your life, and you knew you could not possibly drag yourself from that ungodly habit or association. And in those early moments of triumph you found you had a new power. Whatever that thing was, it fell before the power of Christ — it was your earliest triumph.

I wonder, my dear brother, has the flesh retaken that place of your earliest triumph, the city whose walls fell down flat in the early years of your triumphs for God? Is the place of your earliest triumph the place of your present defeat? and instead of singing the songs of victory, you look back to the fact that God did give you deliverance, but that through indulging the flesh the enemy has retaken the land. You know what I mean

—that man that gave up smoking, that man that gave up drink, that woman who gave up her bad temper or her pride, or some other thing that enslaved before we trusted Christ. And in the moment of triumph and deliverance the Lord gave us the strength to give them up. But in the territory where once we had deliverance, the enemy has raised his standard again. He has retaken the city of palm trees, he has retaken Jericho. And that seems to stand almost as an emblem in this chapter —the enemy, come from Moab. Of course, coming from Moab, they've to come from the east side of the Jordan, they have to cross the Jordan — then Jericho. The enemy from the world's side of things has come in and retaken the ground that once we had gained. There are so many spheres in our lives where many of us have known deliverance from the power of the flesh. Let us ask ourselves in the presence of God: has the enemy retaken territory from which he was once driven?

The King of Moab dominated for eighteen long years until God's people cried unto the Lord for deliverance. Have any of us ever come to the point where we have decided to cry to the Lord for deliverance? Oh! the tragedy of needing to be redelivered. Oh no, you can't get resaved, I don't mean that. But our salvation was a deliverance from this present evil world, and are we losing territory, and do we need to be redelivered? Is there some dear brother looking back on his life and seeing deliverance in the past, but he has given way to the flesh and the enemy has retaken territory? And in your solitary moments in the presence of God your conscience condemns you, and you almost feel like crying "Oh God! if only I could get back" — they cried to the Lord for deliverance. Is there some dear sister, and sometimes your conscience smites you: you're not living for God as you used to do, not so much like the Lord as you used to be, it seems as though the enemy has been gaining territory in your life — ever cried to the Lord for deliverance? "They cried unto the Lord for deliverance, and he raised up a saviour." I like that! And while I have said, and believe, that the judges are a picture of the overseeing brethren, one cannot pass over this remark without mentioning that in the Revised Version the word is "saviour", not deliverer. There is always The Saviour! However much the overseeing brethren may fail, and however much our fellow-saints may fail, there is always The Saviour. In the Hebrew epistle it says, "He is able to save them to the uttermost that come unto God by him, seeing he ever liveth to make intercession for them." And how many of these judges failed? How many of the elder brethren fail in their ministry to God's people? But there is a Saviour, and He never fails to pray. And if we cry unto Him in the desperation of our souls because flesh is regaining territory, we shall find that there is a Saviour. We thank God, we have a High Priest whose ministry is to prevent us from sinning. We have an Advocate whose ministry is to recover us when we do sin. And the Saviour said in John chapter 17, "For this cause I set apart myself, that they might be set apart through the truth." There is raised up a Saviour.

We are going to look, however, at the saviour as representing the elders, and in a broad sense representative of all of us in this battle which we must fight in order that we might have victory over the flesh and drive it out of our territory and subdue it beneath our feet. God raised up Ehud. His name means "joining

3

together". When God's people grieve Him, fellowship is not enjoyed. I can't say fellowship is broken because "our fellowship is with the Father and with his Son Jesus Christ," but the enjoyment of that fellowship we may lose. When the flesh regains territory in our lives and sin becomes a feature in our living, it always comes in between. Sin always breaks communion. Sin always brings in a cloud, always brings in a sense of distance. But here is a man joining together. It's a grand thing when you can join the saints together. But it's an even grander thing when some dear saint has a cloud between him and the Lord, and you can move the cloud away, and join together.

My dear fellow elders, you will have had experience of this. I think you will agree that it is a holy moment in Christian experience when you go and spend a little time with a saint who has allowed some cloud to come in between his soul and the Lord, and through reading the Scriptures and praying together you see the cloud taken away. You see the dear brother on his knees in tears talking to the Lord — maybe he hasn't talked to Him for a while — and you join them together. That's good, isn't it? That's overseers' work. To apply this individually for a moment: maybe there's a dear child of God with a cloud between himself and the Lord. You know what that cloud is. I don't need to tell you. Would you like to be joined together? Would you like to look up and realise a Father's smile, like to feel at home again in the presence of God, instead of having a guilty conscience? Ehud — joined together. There's nothing like it, you know. When a prodigal saint returns home, he feels the Father's arms as He runs and falls on his neck and kisses him.

This man Ehud the son of Gera was a Benjamite, a man left-handed. No, it's not left-handed in the ordinary sense: the word means "shut of his right hand". Did he have a right hand which once he could use but somehow, perhaps through an accident or paralysis, he was "shut of his right hand"? He wasn't naturally left-handed, but he had to use it because he "was shut of his right hand". He was also a Benjamite. What is that? "Son of my right hand". It was his spiritual privilege to be a son of the right hand; and as a son of the right hand he had a place of elevation, a place of multi-privilege. As a son of the right hand he was honoured, if you like, and should have enjoyed heavenly things. But here was a strange thing — a son of the right hand, but his right hand couldn't grasp. Something had gone wrong with it. I'm glad that is the man that God used, because you see, I am a son of the right hand. I'm blessed with all spiritual blessings in the heavenlies in Christ; God has given me a place of elevation, a place of honour, a place of enjoyment of the very highest of spiritual truths. But so often "I'm shut of the right hand", and fail to live in the good of my honoured position. I'm a son of the right hand who has often lost his grip on divine things and never grasped them as I should. Is that not where most of the saints are?

You talk to the saints of God about Ephesian truths today and they say, "It's alright, brother, living in the heavenlies, but I'm conscious of being so much on earth. It's alright talking about living in the heavenlies but if you knew the job I do, and if you knew my heart — oh! living in the heavenlies." But that's what we are: sons of the right hand that have lost our grip, not living up to what is ours in Christ. In the Ephesian epistle you've got

all the right-hand things in chapters 1, 2 and 3 — that's
the doctrinal part of the epistle — "all our spiritual
blessings in the heavenlies in Christ." And then in
chapter 4 you have a look at the assembly from the
heavenlies. My dear brother, men of the right hand,
look at the assembly from the heavenlies, and it's a
wonderful place.

The apostle proceeds to look at the relationships of
husbands and wives, from the heavenlies. I tell you even
married life is better when you look at it from the
heavenlies. How does the husband love his wife? Just as
Christ loved the church. How does the wife reverence
her husband? Just how the church should reverence
Christ. Married life is wonderful from the heavenlies.

Ephesians looks at the parents and children; and the
relationships between parents and children are elevated
when you look at them from the heavenlies. Then there
are masters and servants; that also becomes elevated
when you look at it from the heavenlies. And you and I
should be men and women who look at things from the
divine angle. But, you see, we are like Ehud: we are
"shut of the right hand". All of us have to admit that we
live very low as far as spiritual things are concerned, and
living like that we ask "can we ever possibly have victory
over the flesh?" And for our encouragement it's a man
like that, a man "shut of the right hand" — Ehud —
who subdues Eglon.

My dear brother, as I view Calvary and all that it
means, it touches my conscience to its very core, when I
remember that every time I succumb to the flesh, I am
allowing to live the thing that Christ died to put away.
It's always good to have a look at the death of Christ,
and remember that every time I sin Christ suffered for

EHUD — THE DIPLOMAT

that sin upon the cross. Have we sinned today? Think seriously! Two thousand years ago upon a Roman gibbet the Lord Jesus suffered for the sins you and I have committed today.

Ehud seems to be a man of high position, a government representative, a diplomat. Notice he is literally associated with "cloak and dagger". It is written that by him the children of Israel sent a present unto Eglon. This was doubtless tribute money demanded by Eglon when he had defeated the children of Israel. The payment, possibly in kind, was so large that it needed a number of people (v. 18), to bear it. When Ehud was preparing for his mission, this man whom God had raised up to be a saviour of His people, we read that he "made him a dagger [sword, R.V.] which had two edges." What a picture of the word of God. "The word of God is quick and powerful, and sharper than any two-edged sword" (Hebrews 4:12). "The sword of the Spirit, which is the word of God" (Ephesians 6:17). Are we not being taught again that the only weapon the Lord has given to us in the battle against the world, the flesh and the devil is the word of God? Ehud made him a dagger, and we need to make the word of God our very own: "Thy words were found and I did eat them; and thy words were me the joy and rejoicing of mine heart" (Jeremiah 15:16). This dagger was of a cubit length — a complete measurement. Not a little bit less than a cubit, nor a little bit more than a cubit. If the dagger would remind us of the word of God to be used against the flesh, let us ever remember it must be the whole of the word of God, nothing more and nothing less. How easy to spare the flesh by ignoring, leaving out, not reading the parts of the word of God that we do not

want to obey! Some believers ignore some parts of the
word of God. Some explain away certain sections, argue
that they were not meant for the day in which we live,
were only applicable to backward, uneducated, primitive
peoples. How subtle are our hearts — deceitful,
desperately wicked. Some even go the length of taking
advantage of the ignorance of ordinary saints by saying
that on certain passages the manuscripts are not clear!
Oh, for honest Ehuds! A whole cubit please, my dear
fellow saints. Let us take the whole book, and in the
divine presence apply its keen edge to our conscience.
Let us not forget that we must not add to the cubit — not
God's word plus our ideas, prejudices, traditions. Do not
add to the word of God because you like things done a
certain way. Phariseeism loves to add to the word of God
its burdensome traditions. Let us then take the whole of
the word of God — nothing added, nothing omitted,
deviation neither to the right hand nor the left — and
apply it not so much to others but to that flesh that hides
within our breasts.

The sacred record continues, "He hid it under his
raiment upon his right thigh." It was hidden under his
clothes, attached to his right leg. Simple in application,
is it not? "Thy word have I hid in my heart that I might
not sin against thee" (Psalm 119:11). Do we not need to
hide the word in our hearts, have it in our minds, so that
the Spirit may bring it to our minds in hours of crisis
when the flesh tempts — that we might not sin against
the Lord? Will you please notice it was attached to his
right leg. (Easy to be used by the left hand.) His right
thigh — the idea of power and strength to walk. His leg
and the dagger would move in perfect harmony
together. Oh, that His word and our daily walk would

harmonise in that way. Robed and prepared in this way, he presents the "present" and sends the people that had come with him away.

He does not however proceed immediately to assassinate Eglon, for we read, "But he himself turned back from the quarries that were in Gilgal." A.V. and R.V. margin says "graven images". Many suggestions have been made as to what this refers to — boundary stones, city-state boundary stones mentioned in Ugaritic Akkadian Texts; but the most probable suggestion seems to be: "An easier and more likely explanation is this, that they were the actual stones set up by Joshua to commemorate the miraculous crossing of Jordan (Joshua 4:1-24) and thus were a well-known landmark." (*Judges* by Arthur E. Condall — T Press) The question now arises, "Why should Ehud take a journey to these stones before he deals with Eglon?" and indeed, "Why should he again tarry by the stones, after dealing with Eglon?" Nothing that is recorded in God's word is unneccessary, and therefore we must examine the importance of the incident in Joshua 4 of which these stones are a memorial. The reader would be well advised to turn to Joshua 4 and read carefully the whole chapter.

v. 2 "Twelve men, out of every tribe a man". These men would thus be representative of the twelve tribes — the whole of the nation.

v. 3 "Take you hence out of the midst of Jordan, out of the place where the priests' feet stood firm, twelve stones, and ye shall carry them over with you and leave them in the lodging place where ye shall lodge this night."

v. 8 "And the children of Israel did so as Joshua

commanded, and took up twelve stones out of the midst of the Jordan ... according to the number of the tribes of the children of Israel."

Now notice what Joshua did —

v. 9 "Joshua set up twelve stones in the midst of the Jordan in the place where the feet of the priests which bare the ark of the covenant stood, and they are there unto this day."

In Joshua chapter 3 "the ark of the covenant of the Lord your God" is mentioned in various ways, many times. The ark of the covenant with the mercy seat cannot fail to suggest to us the Person of the Lord Jesus. "He is the propitiation for our sins" (1 John 2:2). "God sent his Son to be the propitiation for our sins" (1 John 4:10). "Christ Jesus, whom God set forth to be a propitiation, through faith, by His blood" (Romans 3:25, R.V.). The gold of the ark overlaying the wood reminds us of absolute Godhood and perfect humanity united together in one unique Person.

It is instructive to notice that when the ark moved forward the word was, "Yet there shall be a space between you and it, about two thousand cubits by measure: come not near unto it" (Josh. 3:4). There always must and always will be a vast space between the ark and the people, between the infinite and the finite, between the wonder and excellence of the Person of Christ, God with us, and ourselves, the objects of divine grace. Surely "in all things he might have the pre-eminence." It is the ark that preceded them into Jordan, picture of the Person of Christ descending into the waters of judgment on our behalf. However, the priests that bore the ark went into the depth of the Jordan along with the ark, and while the ark with the priests remained there "all the people passed clean over Jordan."

Now to return to the lesson of the stones. First, twelve stones, representative of the twelve tribes, went down into the Jordan; then, twelve stones came up out of the Jordan and were set up as a memorial.

After the ark came up out of the Jordan the waters of Jordan returned unto their place. The people had been associated with the ark in the depth of the Jordan, and these stones in the Jordan were left there as a memorial of them. In picture we view ourselves as associated with Christ in His death. Should we not say that at the Red Sea we learn the glorious truth that "Christ died for me," but at the Jordan we learn a further truth: "I died with Christ." So Colossians 2:20 says "If [since] ye died with Christ from the rudiments of the world, why as though living in the world do ye subject yourselves to ordinances?" We died with Christ. Like the stones in the bottom of the Jordan we have been associated with Christ in His death. As it were, like the stones, we are in the bottom of Jordan, in the place of death, the end of myself, the end of my flesh in the death of Christ. Does not the word clearly say, "For what the law could not do, in that it was weak through the flesh, God sending his own Son in the likeness of sinful flesh, and for sin, condemned sin in the flesh" (Romans 8:3)?

There were not only twelve stones down in the Jordan, but twelve stones brought up out of the Jordan. These stones had been where the priests that carried the ark of the Lord had stood, and had now been brought up and erected on the other side of the river of judgment. The New Testament, again in the epistle to the Colossians (3:1): "If ye then be risen with Christ, seek those things which are above, where Christ sitteth on the right hand of God." Let us further note that it was not the same stones that were set up in the midst of the Jordan that were brought up. It was, shall we say, old stones that were set up in Jordan, new stones that were set up on the shore. The old stones represented the whole of the nation in the place of death and judgment in association with the ark; the new stones, the same persons but associated with resurrection. Is not the truth of this contained in Romans 6:3, 4, "So many of us as were baptised into Jesus Christ were baptised into his death; therefore we were buried with him by baptism into death, that like as Christ was raised up from the dead by the glory of the Father, even so we also should walk in newness of life." This surely is the truth that wonderfully fits in our chapter where we learn to deal effectively with the flesh. The end of the flesh, that old nature, is doctrinally seen in the death of Christ. When He died, we died. And it will be to the profit of our souls to visit the place of the stones and recognise that the cross of Christ is the end of me as a man after the flesh. So says the Spirit again in Romans 6, "Likewise reckon ye yourselves to be dead unto sin, but alive unto God, through Jesus Christ our Lord."

Shall we also consider that these stones were at Gilgal which eloquently tells the same story: "At that time the Lord said unto Joshua, Make thee sharp knives and circumcise again the children the second time." Gilgal is the place of the sharp knives, for the cutting off of the flesh. The fact that this is said to be the second time reminds us that the sharp knife of the word of God should once and again be applied to the thing within us called the flesh.

Now Ehud comes from the place of the stones. It's

interesting to notice that he went to the place of the stones again after he had killed Eglon. We do sing sometimes, "Jesus, keep me near the cross." Near the cross: it's a good place to live, the place of the end of the flesh. "God forbid that I should glory save in the cross of our Lord Jesus Christ, by whom the world is crucified unto me and I unto the world." A good place to live — it keeps you from sinning. Now says Ehud as he goes into the presence of Eglon, "I have a secret message unto thee." You secretly deal with the flesh. You get into the presence of God about it, you and God alone to deal with the flesh. You'll need to get that great fat Eglon in your life right into the presence of God, with the Word of God.

You know, the sins in our lives are mainly secret, aren't they? Just us and God. Other people don't know anything about them. You'll need to get into the presence of God about them. When others have gone out — now is the time — only Ehud and Eglon alone, only God looking. That is the way to deal with sin. There in the presence of God to spread it out, in all its fatness, like Eglon. Eglon is before him; I don't want to be too crude, but he talks about his belly and the filth. That's the way to deal with sin in the presence of God — spread it out. Then he said, "I have a message from God unto thee." That's it — he goes in secret, and then a message from God to him.

It is necessary to get alone with God to deal with the flesh. "If we confess our sins, he is faithful and just to forgive us our sins and to cleanse us from all unrighteousness" (1 John 1:9). "I acknowledged my sin unto thee, and mine iniquity have I not hid. I said, I will confess my transgressions unto the Lord, and thou forgavest the iniquity of my sin" (Psalm 32:5).

Why, if someone should read this and get into God's presence to deal secretly with the Eglon in their lives, what a message from God, what a smiting of flesh! And I tell you, when you smite the flesh, what the Authorised Version says will come true (whether it's the right translation or not may be questioned, but what it says will be true): when you put the knife of the Word of God right through the flesh the dirt will come out, and you'll see the flesh is far more obnoxious as it lies revealed in all its filth, than ever you thought it was. Could not Paul declare, "For I know that in me, that is, in my flesh, dwelleth no good thing."

When Ehud had dealt with Eglon he said to the people of God, "Follow after me." Dear elder brother, this is for you now, as an elder. This is for me, as an elder in my local assembly. Have you dealt with the flesh? have you mortified it in your own life? does it lie dead with all its filth exposed and dealt with secretly in the presence of God? Dear brother, if you have done that you are in a moral condition to stand before God's people and say, "Follow me," and lead God's people to deal effectively with the flesh.

Notice please they dealt with the flesh and they slew of the flesh ten thousand men, and they were all, as we have already said, ridiculously fat men, but they were all men who could fight. And every one of us has got a ridiculously fat man living inside us — the Moab principle — and it can fight desperately to retain its power and dominance in our lives. So elders must lead, and the people must follow, and we must, all of us, deal with the flesh. You'll notice what it says: "So Moab was subdued." Now that's interesting. Different things happened against different enemies. Against Chushan-rishathaim — they prevailed. Against Moab — it was subdued. Jabin was discomfited — then destroyed. But notice please that Moab is not destroyed. You'll never destroy Moab as long as you live. He's like Amalek: he lives on. All you can do with Moab is subdue him. This means constant vigilance every day of our lives to keep the Moab principle down. We must subdue and subdue, and Ehud managed to subdue it for eighty years. The Lord help us to do so.

The Minor Judges

Let us now consider the little men, the minor judges of the Book of Judges. There are altogether fifteen judges, thirteen of them in the Book of Judges, two of them in the First Book of Samuel. Thirteen judges: that's an interesting number, the number of rebellion, and marks off the Book of Judges as the book of rebellion. A day when there was no king in Israel and every man did that which was right in his own eyes. Among these thirteen judges there are seven big men and six little men. We have dealt with several of the big men, we will now consider the little men. Most of us are little men, aren't we?

If they had lived in our day, the world would never have noticed them. They were just little men. So much little men, that of some of them you get the idea that they were born in a certain street, lived in the same street, died in the same street, and were buried in the same street. People who had never got beyond their own doorstep. We haven't many of those little men alive today, have we? But when you older folk were young you'll remember it was quite an adventure to go far from home. In those days there were overseers in the assemblies and some of them had not been outside the town in which they lived. As far as the world was concerned they were little unknown men. So in the Book of Judges you have little men like that.

One lovely thing we shall see about those little men is this, that with the exception of Shamgar, there was peace when these little men judged God's people. I

suppose it's always the big men that bring the trouble
and always the big men that lead saints astray. Men of
prominence, men of self-importance, men of worldly
influence often bring in difficulties. With little men
among God's people, ordinary men, self-effacing men,
quiet men, you generally have peace among God's
people. So there are five men just like that. And
Shamgar, another very ordinary man, makes up the six
people who were little.

SHAMGAR

Let us look first of all at this man called Shamgar. You
find him in Judges chapter 3 and verse 31. "After him
was Shamgar the son of Anath, which slew of the
Philistines six hundred men with an ox-goad: and he
also delivered Israel." Here is a very ordinary character.
Someone has said he was a peasant; that might be true.
In our country he might be called a farm labourer. Just a
Shamgar, a man with an ox-goad. You notice he slew six
hundred Philistines, but he didn't use a sword — he
wasn't a soldier. He wasn't, to use another biblical term,
a man of war from his youth. He was just a farm
labourer, used to dealing with stubborn oxen, and he
was one of the men God raised up in the midst of His
people. And it says, "He also delivered Israel." That
"also" is interesting, isn't it? Because Othniel delivered
Israel, and Ehud delivered Israel, and now he also. So
the Spirit of God mentions this unknown character
Shamgar, has lifted him up and put him on the same
platform as Othniel the soldier and Ehud the diplomat.
For Othniel had proved himself as a man who was
valiant in using a sword and taking cities. Ehud was the

man who was sent at the head of an official delegation by the people of Israel to pay the year's tribute to Eglon, so he must have been a very powerful diplomat. So there are two great men. But the Spirit of God lifts this ordinary farm labourer and He says, "He also delivered Israel."

In the things of God one does not need to be great in valour or prowess, or a clever man, a trained diplomat, possibly a man who is a linguist. Oh no! you don't need to be that when it comes to divine things. When it comes to shepherding an assembly, you don't need a powerful man as this world judges. What you need is a man raised up of God, to be a deliverer of God's people. Shamgar couldn't use a sword, and I suppose if he was just a peasant or a farm labourer he could hardly speak his own language properly, yet he was raised up, and it says that he also delivered Israel. That means there is hope for all us men, because we are not much better, if any better, than dear Shamgar. There are none of us valiant men in war, and I suppose most of us are not very well educated, and we are not very clever. But when it comes to delivering God's people from the various kinds of spiritual enemies that would oppose them, you don't need to be strong in the world's things and you don't need to be very clever. You need to have what Shamgar had — a love for God's people, a love for God's land, and a very real hatred for everything that was against God. So Shamgar looked on Philistines, the enemies of God, and he was raised up of God to deliver Israel.

Now Shamgar is a strange name. It is not Israelitish, nor in any way Jewish; some have considered that he was a Kenite. Both his name and his father's name are not Jewish at all — they are Gentile names. So this man who is raised up to be a deliverer of God's people is a Gentile. Well, it's a wonderful thing to see a Gentile in among the people of God. It's a wonderful thing to see a Gentile brought in to be a leader among the people of God. That's the wonder of the Ephesian epistle: Gentiles brought in among the people of God. While in the early church in Jerusalem I suppose all the elders there would be Jews, as I go through the New Testament I don't find that all the elders were Jews and all the ordinary folk were Gentiles. That would be the position, wouldn't it, in Old Testament philosophy? and that will be the position in the coming days after the church has been raptured heavenward. Blessing to Israel, and blessing to the Gentiles in subordination to Israel. But in the church there are Gentile believers. And there is not only the wonder of them being brought in, but brought in to take a place of leadership in the assemblies of God's people. So that when I go to the churches in the Acts of the Apostles I find that the divine centre shifts from Jerusalem to Antioch. In Antioch there are Gentile overseers, one of the first places where I find prophets and teachers who are afterwards called overseers; there they are and there are Gentiles among them. So we have this idea of those who are Gentiles brought in. Firstly the wonderful privilege of being among the people of God, but equally wonderful that among the people of God, those who were originally Gentiles are now leaders of the people of God.

Thirdly, I find that this man's name, Shamgar, means pilgrim and stranger; and of course not only are the overseers amongst us pilgrims and strangers, but all of us. Through divine grace we have been separated from this world altogether. Having in spirit crossed the Red

4

Sea, we have embarked on the wilderness, and we are passing through this world as pilgrims going home, as strangers away from home. So all the saints of God can take their place alongside Shamgar. Of course, it is very important, isn't it, if you are an overseer in an assembly to remember that all the people of God are pilgrims and strangers, and you must remember too, my dear brother, that you are a pilgrim and a stranger. What a tragedy it can be for an assembly if you have an overseer or overseers who have forgotten that they must hold the things of the world with a loose hand; and instead of being in pilgrim character, they settle down as if they were earth-dwellers, and all they can think of is worldly things and worldly methods and worldly advancement. If you have overseers who have forgotten their pilgrim character it is a very sorry day for the people of God. So every one of us must remember we are pilgrims and strangers, we are merely passing through, we do not belong here.

Notice please that Shamgar was fighting against the Philistines. This is the first time we get these men in the Book of Judges. Who are they? The Philistines very likely originated in the islands of the Mediterranean and eventually crossed to Egypt. Then they just wandered on until they came into what we call Palestine, but whose original name was Philistia. They wandered into the land where the Word of God says "God had placed his name," and "his eye rests upon it from the beginning of the year unto the end." They were never in bondage. They never made bricks and built cities, as slaves in Egypt. The judgments of God never fell upon Egypt because of the Philistines. There never was a night when in their homes they were sheltered by blood. There never was a morning when they left their houses to make their way towards the Red Sea. The Philistines never passed through the Red Sea on dry ground. They never came up the other side to stand on redemption ground and sing redemption's song. No! They started in Egypt, they came into the land, but they had never known the lash and never been sheltered by blood and never been delivered from the world and never become pilgrims and strangers. God's people Israel were different. They also started in Egypt, didn't they? But they knew the lash, they knew what it was to be sheltered by blood, knew what it was to be delivered by power. They passed through the Red Sea and sang the song of redemption. They were pilgrims and strangers. But notice, they both started in the same place and they both finished in the same place.

What then is the difference between the Philistines and the people of God? Look all around you in Christendom: you know very well that all those people belong to Egypt, that's where they started. Just as sure as you and I started in an Egypt world. But where are they? In all kinds of religious buildings that take the name of God and all kinds of religious denominations that take the name of Christian. They have God's name and they call themselves churches, and therefore profess they are in the place where God has placed His name. They started in Egypt, and they are in the sphere where God's name is and Christ's name is. So much so that they profess to be churches, and broadly speaking you call them Christendom: they've got the name of Christ on them. Where did you and I start? Well, we started in Egypt too, and we take the name of Christ. Then what is the difference? The Israelites felt the lash, i.e. they felt the burden of the bondage, the burden of their sins, the burden of their position. The Philistines never felt that. In other words, true believers have known the conviction of sin and longed to be delivered. Philistines have never known the conviction of sin and never longed to be forgiven. God's people, a picture of you and I as Christians, look back to a night when we realised that we were sheltered by the blood. There are thousands of people in Christendom and if you talk to them about the need to be sheltered by blood, they would say, You mean I need to be saved like those drunkards? As for blood, what an obnoxious idea to talk about being washed in the blood! They would reject that altogether. You see, that is the difference. Both Philistines and Israelites started in the same place, but one nation knew the lash and the other didn't. One nation knew redemption by blood and the other didn't. The one nation knew what it was to come through the Red Sea on dry land and the other just wandered through somehow. That's the difference!

So when you look around Christendom today you see people in places with God's name on it, they say it is Christian: but they have arrived there without ever having the conviction of sin, without ever being redeemed by blood, without ever being born again. As for being delivered from this present evil world, they are perfectly at home in it. They don't believe in being pilgrims and strangers, but they profess to be in God's land. That's the Philistines in contradistinction to the people of God.

The Philistines are the common enemy of God's people. We look at them again when we come to Samson. Lovely people, beautiful people, people who

say they know the name of God and take the name of
Christ. But they've never been convicted of their sins,
they've never been sheltered by blood, never been born
again. They are possibly the greatest danger to God's
people that exists in the world. Nice people, refined
people, Christianised people, religious people —
Philistines. Always a danger to God's people. Samson
married them, put his head in the lap of one of them.
Shamgar, he took up an ox-goad and he killed six
hundred of them. Listen my dear brother, my dear
sister, are you a Shamgar or a Samson? Samson, oh yes!
he was a great man, he was a strong man. This man
Shamgar — an unknown insignificant character, but he
had no intention of compromising with the Philistines.
He knew the difference between a true child of God and
an enemy of God. He knew the difference between the
people who belonged to the land and the people who
had just wandered in. He took an ox-goad against the
Philistines. Why?

Look please in chapter 5. Circumstances were the
same as in the days of Jael. What were they like? Well,
the highways were unoccupied. There were main roads,
they were places where you could be attacked by raiders
or robbers. The Philistines, they were there; they were
blocking the road, they were ambushing. The Philistines
were cutting off the liberty of the people of God to go
backwards and forwards. Verse 7 says, "The inhabitants
of the villages ceased, they ceased in Israel." What does
that mean? It means that instead of people living in
villages, where they would be open to attack from the
Philistine hordes which were going from place to place,
they thought the best thing they could do was to collect
themselves together in towns and get some defence

around themselves. So the people lost their liberty, because of the Philistines.

Don't Philistines rob God's people of liberty today? I remember hearing of dear old W.W. Fereday on one occasion. When he was in London he went into St. Paul's Cathedral — a lovely building, plenty to see. The old man was having a look around and he suddenly realised that they were about to commence a service, so he made his way to the door as quickly as he could go and waited for the rest of the folks to come out. Out of the building came a lady and seeing the old man there she said, "Mr. Fereday, don't you think that was a lovely service?" He replied, "My dear woman, that man is being paid to come in between your soul and God." Philistines! robbing God's people of their liberty to go into the presence of God, putting a human priest in between. Philistines! robbing God's people of going out to evangelise in the gospel, for you must have a man who wears the cloth to do that. How many places there are in Christendom today where God's people, many of them, sit in misery on the benches while unconverted men rob them of what is their priestly privileges!

What did Shamgar do? Well, he just took an ox-goad. Was there not a sword? Maybe there were a few swords, but Deborah in her song says, "Then there was war in the gates: was there a shield or a spear seen among the forty thousand of Israel?" Maybe that was why this dear man didn't try to get a sword. You say, a blundering method, an unskilled method, an untrained method. How many of us are unskilled men in using the sword of the Spirit! For many of us it's an ox-goad. We're not warriors, not men skilled in the art of using a sword. Many an overseer in an assembly is an unlearned and unlettered man! His English may be very faulty and his knowledge of the original languages absolutely nil. Sometimes he has to sit down with a dear young Christian and show him from the Book, baptism, gathering to the Name of the Lord Jesus, the truth of the Lord's supper, the priesthood of all believers. And he's like Shamgar: a very ordinary man. Perhaps the person who is being taught will go back to their minister — he's the man who has got a sword, isn't he? He's the man who has got the polish, and it will be the knowledge of a Shamgar that's pitted against the Philistines. But if Shamgar knows how to use his ox-goad he can triumph against the Philistines. Many an ordinary overseer in the assembly of God's people doesn't know anything about the original languages, but he does know his Acts of the Apostles and he does know the first epistle to the Corinthians and he does know what the early saints of God did. So, in a very elementary way as a man who knows how to use an ox-goad — a very ordinary weapon — he can take up the Bible and use it in that simple way and overcome the Philistines.

Many a young Christian has come back from an interview with one of the Philistines, perfectly convinced that the Shamgar in the assembly is a man of God who knows his book and all the philosophical arguments of the other man are of no avail at all. In the part of the country where I preached for the first ten years of my preaching life most of the overseeing brethren were farm labourers. But they did an excellent job and they built in that day excellent assemblies. Men whose hands were hard and corny with the old fashioned methods of farming, but these Shamgars were men who knew how to use the Book.

TOLA

Now turn over please to the next little judge; you'll find him in Judges chapter 10. The context in which you find this man is very, very interesting. The preceding chapter is a very long chapter numbering altogether fifty-seven verses: fifty-seven verses of destruction among God's people; fifty-seven verses of civil war until the people slew the leader and the leader slew the people — absolute devastation. What would you do in an assembly where that was the case? An assembly where the overseers were carnal; so carnal, you wonder if they ever were saved. An assembly where you have a rebel in the meeting and you wonder if ever he was saved. The people of God are all suspicious of each other — on the top of the mountains spying on each other. If the assembly where you fellowship were like that it would be an awful place, with unspiritual overseers against the assembly, and then someone rising up in the assembly, equally unspiritual, and leading a revolt against them. That leads to chaos among the people of God, and at the end of chapter 9 it is just that. When Abimelech was dead and many of the people of God were dead, the rest of them went back to their homes almost in shame, and must have realised the awful trouble the three years of Abimelech's reign had brought among God's people.

When there has been division and trouble among God's people, some falling out with each other, some folks leaving and others rebelling, it leaves the saints of God in an awfully exhausted state. Then God in His providential dealings takes away the men that cause the trouble. That's what happens in Judges chapter 9. The assembly is left weakened, exhausted, divided, and

somebody has got to do something about it; for those
exhausted people are the sheep of God's pasture and
they need a shepherd. So I read that after Abimelech,
after all the trouble, after all the fighting, after God
stepped in and took the people home that were causing
the trouble, after that there arose to defend Israel, Tola,
Judges 10:1.

A lovely man, this one. His name means "a worm".
Could you have anyone more opposite to Abimelech
than a worm? Abimelech, who in one day ceremoniously
slaughtered the seventy sons of Gideon and shed blood
all over the country, but now God has removed him.
God raises up a man (can you use the word 'raise' up?
he's only a worm). This man hardly gets above the
ground; there's no elevation about this man, no pride
about him; he's right down in the dust. It almost
reminds me of the lovely expression of Psalm 22, "I am a
worm, and no man; a reproach of men, and despised of
the people." When you link the two together you get a
lovely idea, don't you, of a man who was an imitation of
Christ, following what the Lord Jesus was. The Lord
Jesus was so low, a worm and no man, reproached,
despised. God raises up a man, Tola, of Christlike
character. In an assembly that was so torn with division
as they were in chapter 9, that's the type of man you
would need among God's people. Not an ostentatious
character, not a proud or a forceful character, but a man
who would just move like a worm, humble, lowly, ready
to be despised, willing to be trodden on. A man like that
to move among God's people to bring peace.

That again takes you back to the Philippian epistle:
meek, lowly, self-sacrificing, humbling oneself, just
worm-like. We think of Christ who humbled Himself to

cross-death: couldn't get lower than that, couldn't be more despised than that. And that's the lovely example for people in the Philippian assembly. Become like that, and all their wars will be over. Become like that, and strife will be gone and they will have peace instead of distress. So when an assembly has gone through days of trouble God can raise up Tolas among His people. My young brother, if you long to be anything among the people of God, long to be a Tola. In every age there's a need for Tola brethren, worm-like brethren, humble brethren, to move and bring peace where Abimelechs have brought war.

Notice please that this man was a man of Issachar; not only a man of Issachar, but he dwelt in Shamir. Of Issachar I read, "He bowed his shoulder to bear, and he became a servant unto tribute." Again I take you in your thinking to the Philippian epistle: He bowed his shoulder to bear, He took upon his shoulder the yoke, He became a bond-servant. Thus Philippians chapter 2 is a lovely example for God's people, the humility and self-giving of Christ a perfect example for the saints to imitate. The man who is going to bring unity after strife will be like a worm moving quietly and humbly, not expecting to be ministered unto but to minister. He'll be a man who takes his place as a slave of the members of the assembly, in order that by his caring for the saints he might bring unity among God's people. He will be Christlike. Note that there is not much of importance said about him except this, "And he judged Israel twenty-three years." I think that's good. You have three years of the trouble of Abimelech (its almost as though God shortened the days, took the man away under His disciplining hand), but the man who followed him, we don't read of anything great that he did or of any battles he fought or of anyone he slew. All he did was maintain peace for twenty-three years among God's people. My dear brother, if you can go home to the glory one day and leave behind an assembly that has had peace for twenty-three years, you'll have done your work well.

JAIR

Now look at the next man. It says, "After him arose Jair, a Gileadite, and judged Israel twenty-two years." Let me repeat again, he never used a sword as far as I know; he never fought a battle; he carried on what Tola had done, and added twenty-two more years of peace among God's people. That's good, isn't it? If you get twenty-three years of peace in the assembly and the dear overseers go home to be with the Lord, are there overseers to take their places to maintain peace among the people of God for another twenty-two years? Two men that did an excellent job: forty-five years of peace among God's people. "Behold how good and how pleasant it is for brethren to dwell together in unity."

Jair means "light-giver". So he's not just moving about worm-like establishing peace where strife had been; he goes a step further now and he is raising the light. One thing to bring peace to God's people, another thing to illumine them, to bring the light of divine truth to them. Instruct them, if you like, lead them. He was a light-giver, light-bearer.

Notice please that Jair, the light-giver, judged Israel for twenty-two years, and he had thirty sons who rode on thirty ass colts. Princes, in the Old Testament, rode on ass colts; it was a sign of their dignity and their rank.

So the New Testament linked with Daniel chapter 9 says, "until Messiah the Prince," and Messiah the Prince entered into Jerusalem riding upon an ass's colt — that's the princely dignity of the Son of God. So these thirty sons were all sons of princely dignity. Do your sons and mine walk with princely dignity? What do they look like? what do they walk like? what do they behave like? Sons of overseeing brethren, "not accused of riot or unruly." Does it say anything about Jair riding on an ass's colt? Presumably he did, but his sons all rode on asses' colts. They were seen going through the countryside with princely dignity. My dear fellow-elders, these sons were a credit to their father, these sons carried the features of their father's dignity; and the children of those who lead God's people should be characterised by princely dignity.

My dear young people, maybe you have not seen the princely dignity that you should see in your fathers. There is a word used in 1 Timothy chapter 2, "That we might lead quiet and peaceable lives in all godliness and gravity." That word gravity is a word that conveys the idea of reverential awe, and teaches that godly men should so walk among God's people that they almost command reverential fear. That's what elders should be like. That's what elders were like when I was a boy. I knew those men, I loved those men. Quite honestly, I was afraid of those men. Not that they were unkind but they had such a sense of godliness. Elder brethren, is there something about you and I that carries the presence of God? something about you and I of the dignity of Heaven? and have our children learned to emulate us? I don't mean being old while they are still young — I loathe young people trying to be old-fashioned — but they should have taken on some of the character of godliness.

You notice something else they did: they had thirty cities. Jair, the Gileadite, he had cities. Then he had thirty sons who had thirty cities, and they were called the cities of Jair. Look it up at your leisure, Numbers 32:41, 1 Chronicles 2:22, and you will find that they started off with twenty-three cities and finished up with thirty cities and several villages added unto that. So the area that was dominated by Jair and his sons was an ever-enlarging sphere; and every city they took over, they made it a replica of the original city, that is, the city of the light-giver. So the thirty sons had thirty cities and they were all "cities of the light-giver". Then they enlarged it to villages beyond that in the Book of Chronicles, and so there was an ever-increasing sphere of giving light.

Think of an assembly with godly overseers and they are all light-givers and they have the privilege of leading younger men to Christ. Now those young people go in their business life to other places, and everywhere they go, they teach what they have been taught. What the practices are in their home assembly are the practices there. As they spread abroad, they carry the light that they saw at the light-giving centre. That is how it is in family life: you rear a family, and soon they go out of the nest. In local assemblies you bring young men to Christ, you teach them, and then they get scattered. That's what it was like in this chapter: thirty sons walking with princely dignity, basking in the light of their father as the light-giver, and then they go abroad and everywhere they go they establish what they learned at home. They spread the light in which they had grown and in which they had been instructed. Here's a good overseer; and the young men among whom he has laboured in the assembly, they have been so illuminated, so instructed, that when they move away they establish in their new sphere the thing they learned at their home assembly, the things you overseers taught them from the Word of God.

IBZAN

In chapter twelve, Jephthah's story concludes by his slaying forty-two thousand of his fellow Israelites. That's what legality will do among God's people. Then in verse 8 you read, "And after him Ibzan of Bethlehem judged Israel. He had thirty sons, and thirty daughters, whom he sent abroad, and took in thirty daughters from abroad for his sons. And he judged Israel seven years. Then died Ibzan, and was buried at Bethlehem." Notice please he seems to have been born in Bethlehem, lived in Bethlehem, died in Bethlehem, and buried in Bethlehem. Bethlehem is a good place to be: it's the house of bread. If you make the assembly a house of bread, my dear brother, you are doing well. (If you were saved in it, lived in it, died in it, and then buried by the dear saints in it.) The house of bread, the place where there was food for the dear saints of God. Is every assembly that? It should be. Every assembly should be a house of bread — that is the responsibility of the overseers: "Feed the flock of God in the which the Holy Ghost hath made you overseers."

My dear brother, you may not be a platform man yourself, but as an overseer you are responsible to see that there is provision made in the assembly for food to feed the people of God. It should be the exercise of overseeing brethren to say to themselves as they gather together, Just what does the assembly need at this particular moment? Have you ever done that? You are responsible to feed as shepherds, you are responsible to lead the saints to the pasture, you are responsible to see on what pasture they are feeding.

Notice also that this man had thirty sons and thirty daughters. And one lovely thing about him: all his sons married, and all his daughters married too. Here was a family, and it seemed as though every family that had a son was delighted when their son married into this family, and every family that had a daughter was delighted when their daughter married into this family. I wonder, my dear brother, my dear sister, is yours the kind of family that other folks would like their family to marry into? It is good when you see your family marrying into Christian families, into homes that are in assembly fellowship, into homes where they love the Lord and fill their time with serving the Lord. Good when you see your children marry into families like that.

If you take these families as pictures of the assembly, is it not good when you see young folk growing up among you and falling in love with others from assemblies which are going on in the ways of God, and you feel they are going to work together in divine things and go on for the glory of God?

Consider too, that he didn't just stay at home with all his sons and his daughters and let them all come to him; it says he sent his daughters abroad. He wasn't just bound up in his own assembly or his own home saying, We'll all live happily together and we'll all be godly together. No! he reared them, and then in a spirit of true evangelism his daughters went abroad to imitate doubtless their mother's kindness, and to remember their father's godliness, and to establish families that would be replicas of the family in which they were reared. I wonder, my dear brother, if your home and mine are like that? Do your children when they marry say, I'd like to build a home like the home in which I was reared?

ELON

The judge who comes next is called Elon. His name means "strength". He judged Israel for ten years, and he was a Zebulonite. What does that mean? Zebulon, you'll remember, was the name given by Leah and she said, "Now will my husband dwell with me." In other words, he was a basis of reconciliation. So he's a strong man, Elon, but he's a man who believes in reconciliation. Is there a man like that in the assembly? You've got a good man — a reconciler. I remember in our home assembly a man called Mr. Reid. He was one of those men who on the platform just talked and talked; just like me. But he was a man of peace, and wherever he went he could put his hand on the shoulders of two arguing brethren and there was peace. Any little ruffle in the assembly, away he went and there was peace. Elon — a strong man, but a man who was a reconciler. Let us read Philippians 4:3, "I beseech thee also, true yoke-fellow, help these women which laboured with me in the gospel" to be reconciled.

ABDON

Finally, Abdon. His name means "service"; son of Hillel, son of praise. That's a lovely man to have in the assembly. A man full of the service of God and a man full of praise. He had forty sons and forty grandsons and they all rode on asses, so there were three generations of princely dignity in his family. They were carrying on their father's service and his praise. Is it not good when you can go three generations in a family (remember that the third generation is often the generation of departure)? But this man could go to his third generation, and they were still princely and dignified.

It says he was a Pirathonite. He lived there, died there, was buried there. A local man with a life of service and praise — what a valuable man in a locality. He was buried there: in the land of Ephraim in the hill country of the Amalekites. That's interesting! The Amalekites were on the hill in Ephraim. One of those enemies keeping the people of God from possessing their possessions. So the Amalekites, the flesh if you like, were on the hill keeping this man down from enjoying his inheritance. But you couldn't keep this man down in the valley, he fought his way up, and he maintained his position on the side of the mountain. Eventually he died and was buried in the hill country. His sepulchre was a monument to this, that he had overcome the Amalekites and taken their territory. If only you and I could die that way, with the words upon our grave "He overcame the Amalekites." "Overcame the flesh."

Jabin, Sisera
Deborah, Barak, Jael

"When Ehud was dead." These are the outstanding words of the opening of chapter 4, and remind us of what chapter 2 has already stated: "When the judge was dead they returned and corrupted themselves more than their fathers." Flesh is incurable, cannot be improved, and once Ehud whose example they had followed in war and peace was removed from them they not only returned to their former ways but waxed worse. Deborah sums up their departure in a poignant phrase in her song, "They chose new gods" which resulted in "then was war in the gates", and in such a situation she asks the question, "Was there a shield or spear seen among forty thousand in Israel?" Apparently a disarmed, defenceless people attacked by an army that carried the battle to the gates of the cities.

Because of the evil of their ways we read again, "The Lord sold them," in His sovereign will putting them under the heel of the oppressor to bring them in repentance back to Himself.

We are now introduced to a new kind of enemy. The first had been from Mesopotamia — a land afar. The second from the land of Moab — nearer home. Both these were in some way related to God's people, both connected to them through Abraham. But this new enemy was in the land, and that before they were, and it would appear had no natural tie with them. Let us examine what the Word of God has to say about him.

First of all, his name. Jabin means "understanding, he is wise, wisdom". He therefore represents a wisdom opposed to God and to His people. James tells us that there is "a wisdom that descendeth not from above, but is earthly, sensual, devilish," and shows us that the wisdom that is the opposite to the wisdom of God finds its origin in the Devil himself.

The New Testament epistles inform us as to the wisdom that is devilish. It would be profitable to read from 1 Corinthians 1:18 to 2:7 and to consider the wisdom that was one of the outstanding features of Corinthian culture, contrasted by the Spirit of God with "Christ, the power of God and the wisdom of God" (v. 24) and again "Christ Jesus, who is made unto us wisdom, righteousness, sanctification and redemption" (v. 30). There is "the wisdom of this world", "wisdom that knew not God", "wisdom after the flesh", "man's wisdom" — all these the wisdom of God hath made foolish. The super-mind behind all this, that old serpent, the devil, constantly trying by his wisdom to oppose the purposes and plans of God. This opposer of God and His saints is the spiritual Jabin of our chapter.

Not only does the Corinthian epistle unveil this enemy but the Colossians saints are also warned, "Beware lest any man spoil you through philosophy and vain deceit, after the tradition of men, after the rudiments of the world, and not after Christ" (2:8). Again, "Let no man beguile you of your reward in a voluntary humility and worshipping of angels ... vainly puffed up by his fleshly mind" (v. 18). The Colossian believers were in danger of being enticed by Judaism, Gnosticism, asceticism, angel worship, planets, feast days, punishing the body, and initiation rites in societies of human wisdom; to embrace these and abandon Christ, or more subtle still, to add these things to Christ. But says the Spirit of God — "Christ, in whom are hid all the treasures of wisdom and knowledge" (2:3). And He answers the challenge of the enemy with the words, "Christ is all, and in all" (3:11).

The two opposing forces are therefore "Christ the wisdom of God" and "the spirit that now worketh in the sons of disobedience".

It seems strange that Jabin appears on first sight to have had such a long and contradictory experience. We read of him in Joshua 11: "Jabin, king of Hazor" (v. 1). "Joshua at that time turned back, and took Hazor, and smote the king thereof with the sword" (v. 10). I take it to mean that Jabin was smitten and died, but he appears again in Judges 4 alive and actively engaged in subjugating the Israelites. It seems that Jabin was a name given to successive kings of Canaan, like 'Abimelech' over the Philistines, 'Pharaoh' in Egypt, 'Herod' in the New Testament. Names held by successive rulers. So we have not the same man, but another man bearing the same name. The Spirit of God has doubtless designed it this way (for these things were written for our learning) to give us the picture of Jabin, slain in battle in Joshua 11:10, but living on, fighting against God's people in Judges 4:1; to be "subdued on that day" (v. 23), and destroyed, "the hand of the children of Israel prospered, and prevailed against Jabin, until they had destroyed Jabin king of Canaan" (v. 24). Herein, I suggest, it is easy to see a picture of Satan, the opposer of the Wisdom of God. (1) Fighting a battle, he was defeated and slain in the past; (2) still living, opposing God's people and being subdued by the saints, in the present time, but (3) being utterly destroyed in the future.

(1) He was defeated in a battle in the past.

"I will put enmity between thee and the woman, and between thy seed and her seed; it shall bruise thy head, and thou shalt bruise his heel" (Genesis 3:15). (His head is bruised, he is mortally wounded but still lives on.)

"... That through death he might destroy him that had the power of death, that is, the devil; and deliver them who through fear of death were all their lifetime subject to bondage" (Hebrews 2:14, 15). The expression rendered in A.V. is variously translated, "annul him" (J.N.D.), "break the power of him" (N.E.B.), "bring to nought" (R.V.), "put a stop" (Williams), "take away the power" (Beck).

The stronger man (the Lord Jesus) has indeed entered into the strong man's house and spoiled his goods! The triumph of Christ is absolutely clear: "Jesus Christ, who is gone into heaven, and is on the right hand of God, angels and authorities and powers being made subject unto him" (1 Peter 3:22).

I think the reader will see that Jabin is meant to portray this picture. But Jabin appears again (after many years) in our chapter; thus we learn that our defeated enemy lives on, still opposing God and His people.

(2) How about the present?

It would be foolish to suggest that the devil is dead, or even because he has been defeated he is bound. He has been mortally wounded, his eternal doom is already assured, but he fights on. Does not Peter say, "Be sober, be vigilant; because your adversary, the devil, as a roaring lion, walketh about, seeking whom he may devour: whom resist steadfast in the faith" (1 Peter 5:8,

9)?

There is abundant evidence in the Scriptures that Satan is very active today. The personal experience of every saint will confirm this. See such expressions as:

"Neither give place to the devil"   Ephesians 4:27
"Resist the devil"   James 4:7
"Lest Satan tempt you"   1 Corinthians 7:5
"Lest Satan should get an
   advantage"   2 Corinthians 2:11
"Satan himself is transformed"   11:14
"A messenger of Satan"   12:7
"Satan hindered"   1 Thessalonians 2:18
"Serpent beguiled Eve"   2 Corinthians 11:3

He was defeated at Calvary but still lives on, and against him God's people have constantly to fight. He has his wiles of subtlety and fiery darts to attack. He appears as both roaring lion and creeping serpent, and we need to be constantly on our guard against him.

It is our business in the present to resist and subdue him by the power of God and the word of God.

(3) But what of the future? for Jabin was in the end utterly destroyed.

Let us examine some passages of the Holy Scripture that are yet to be fulfilled:

(a) "And there was war in heaven: Michael and his angels fought against the dragon; and the dragon fought and his angels, and prevailed not; neither was their place found anymore in heaven. And the great dragon was cast out, that old serpent, called the Devil, and Satan, which deceiveth the whole world, he was cast out into the earth and his angels were cast out with him ... the accuser of our brethren is cast down, which accused them before our God day and night ... Woe to the inhabiters of the earth and of the sea for the devil is come down onto you, having great wrath, because he knoweth that he hath but a short time" (Revelation 12:7-12).

This event takes place in the middle of the seventieth week of Daniel's prophecy, that is, at the beginning of the Great Tribulation. From this time onward his activities are confined to the earth.

(b) "And I saw an angel come down out of heaven, having the key of the bottomless pit and a great chain in his hand. And he laid hold on the dragon ... and bound him a thousand years, and cast him into the bottomless pit, and shut him up, and put a seal upon him, that he should deceive the nations no more, till the thousand years should be fulfilled, after that he must be loosed a little season. And I saw thrones and they sat upon them and judgment was given unto them ... And they lived and reigned with Christ a thousand years" (Revelation 20:1-8).

This refers to the one thousand years reign of Christ, the Millennium.

(c) "And when the thousand years are expired, Satan shall be loosed out of his prison, and shall go out to deceive the nations ... and they went up on the breadth of the earth, and compassed the camp of the saints about, and the beloved city, and fire came down from God out of heaven and devoured them. And the devil which deceived them was cast into the lake of fire and brimstone, where the beast and the false prophet are and shall be tormented day and night for ever and ever." (Revelation 20:7-10)

Thus like the Jabin of our chapter he will be finally utterly destroyed in the lake of fire.

Let us turn again to Joshua chapter 11 to learn some more details relative to Jabin.

(a) He occupied the land before God's people sought to possess it.

(b) He was king of Hazor, and Hazor beforetime was the head of all those kingdoms (v. 10).

(c) He had under him a number of subordinate kings and their armies (v. 10).

(d) The cities he had rule over were all standing in their strength (A.V.) on their mounds (v. 13).

We shall take up these points and apply them to the spiritual Jabin, Satan himself.

(a) We have already seen according to Revelation 12 he has a place in the heavenlies until he is cast down in the middle of the seventieth week of Daniel.

(b) He is the prince of the power of the air, the spirit that now worketh in the sons of disobedience.

(c) He has under him subordinate enemies, called "principalities, powers, world rulers of this darkness, spiritual wickedness in the heavenly places."

(d) All these in the air, heavenly places are on their mounds.

Notice also "Jabin had nine hundred chariots of iron." The forces of the children of Israel were ground troops fighting the conventional battles of their day. But Jabin had forces that were stronger and higher, they were above the ordinary soldiers (there were no planes in that day). These forces fighting from chariots above ordinary soldiers represent the strength of those beings we have already referred to, spiritual powers in the heavenliess ready to attack God's people. What is then before us is not a battle against flesh and blood, but a battle fought by powers above men — a spiritual conflict. In order to fight against Jabin and his chariots Israel would need also to be equipped with spiritual power, thus we shall see Barak from Kedesh-naphtali means a wrestler in the sanctuary to harness spiritual power. Deborah's song helps to illuminate our minds on this subject when she declares:

> "They fought from heaven;
> The stars in their courses fought against Sisera.
> The river Kishon swept them away,
> The ancient river, the river Kishon.
> O my soul, march on with strength.
> Then were the horsehoofs broken
> By means of the pransings,
> The pransings of their mighty ones."

Thus Deborah recognises that in the meeting and defeating of these forces of Jabin it was God fighting on their behalf from heaven. We are instructed, "Be strong in the Lord and in the power of his might ... ye shall be able to quench all the fiery darts of the wicked one" (Ephesians 6:10-16).

The captain of the host of Jabin was Sisera, whose name means "battle array". He would be responsible for the deployment of his men upon the field of battle. Jabin as we have seen represents him who is the prince of the power of the air, Satan, a person. But the Ephesian epistle adds, "the spirit that now worketh in the sons of disobedience." So while there is a spiritual enemy in the heavenlies with his subordinate wicked spirits, there is also an enemy on earth. Satan has his army, his servants on earth to carry out his plans. Thus the battle is set in array.

The apostle Paul speaks of the strategy of the enemy in 2 Corinthians 11 thus: "But I fear, lest by any means, as the serpent beguiled Eve through his subtlety, so your minds should be corrupted from the simplicity and the purity that is toward Christ" (R.V.). Continuing in that vein, he speaks of those whom the adversary uses for this work as "the very chiefest of the apostles" (he again refers to them in that way in chapter 12, verse 11). Again he continues after a verse or two, "For such are false apostles, deceitful workers, transforming themselves into the apostles of Christ. And no marvel, for Satan himself is transformed into an angel of light. Therefore it is no great thing if his ministers also be transformed as the ministers of righteousness; whose end shall be according to their works" (11:13-15). Peter and Jude and John will confirm these warnings about the servants of Satan operating among the people of God. John says, "Many deceivers are gone forth into the world, even they that confess not that Jesus Christ is come in the flesh" (2 John 7). In other words, the battle is set in array and satanic forces are on the move attacking the minds of the people of God.

And so from Harosheth of the Gentiles, meaning "artifice of the nations" (Chaldee: In the strength of the citadel of the nations) the battle is joined against the children of Israel.

For twenty long years Jabin and his forces mightily oppressed the children of Israel, and then Deborah, a prophetess and judge, arose.

THE DESTRUCTION OF JABIN

Deborah was not the only woman that prophesied in

the Scriptures. Women like Miriam, Huldah, Mary and old Anna used their voices for God.

Even in the Acts of the Apostles the idea of a prophetess is not foreign to the New Testament scriptures. For while a woman is told clearly in the Scriptures she must not speak in the assembly and commanded to be in silence, yet Philip had four daughters that prophesied. They did not prophesy in the assembly, they did not prophesy to the apostle, neither did they prophesy to the young associates of the apostle. God had a message for the apostle Paul but sent Agabus down to Jerusalem to deliver it.

While it is true that there were prophetesses in the Old Testament scriptures, it never seems to be in the divine mind that womenfolk should be in the position of rule. The Book of Judges says that God raised up Othniel, God raised up Ehud, the angel of the Lord appeared to Gideon, and the angel of the Lord appeared to Manoah and his wife. It doesn't say that God raised up Deborah. Deborah seems to be among the people who raised up themselves. But God used her. Abimelech raised up himself. Jephthah raised up himself. We should not be surprised, for there was no king in Israel and every man did that which was right in his own eyes. Even so when one examines the history of Christendom from post-apostolic days to the days in which we live — days characterised by this feature: no king in Israel and every man doing that which is right in his own eyes — one will find professed companies of Christians where unconverted men raise up themselves as leaders of the professed people of God. Are there not places in Christendom led by women who raised themselves up to leadership, which God's word forbids?

Deborah lived in a day when men abysmally failed and there was no one apparently among them fit to judge. A woman was the one to whom they sought for guidance in such tragic days. It was a woman to whom the Lord communicated His mind, as a prophetess, to encourage a cowardly man to go out and lead God's people. Deborah acting as both prophetess and judge was surely a condemnation of all the men of that day. And if a woman needed to go and tell Barak that the Lord had already told him to go ("hath not the Lord said?"), he was not only deaf to the voice of God but disobedient to what he had heard, and so the raising up of Deborah was to his condemnation. Maybe even in our day when God uses women it is to the condemnation of men.

What would you men do if a woman rose up in the meeting on Lord's day morning and took part? You say that the brethren would talk to her after the meeting and explain to her. Would not her action be to the condemnation of some of the men in the meeting? You see, we live in a day when some women are wanting the place that Scripture has given to men. But did you ever think about the men who remain silent and act like women? The New Testament says, "I will that men pray." How many men are there whose voices have never been heard in prayer or worship since they came into assembly fellowship, never given out a hymn, and never read the Scriptures? They are acting as though they were women. Please don't say I am justifying women taking part in the meeting — I'm not! I teach against it. But brother, are you taking up the privilege that God has given you in the New Testament scriptures? Listen! if all the men behaved as you do there would not be a meeting; but some of the men are perfectly content to remain silent year after year.

The Epistle to the Hebrews commenting on the period of the judges reads, "By faith ... Gideon, Samson, Jephthah, David ..." and in among them Barak — not Deborah.

As a prophetess she did two things: she encouraged Barak and she had a message from God for him; she also wrote a song. And both her encouragement of Barak and her song are found in the Holy Scriptures.

Notice please verses 6 and 7 of chapter 5. This is part of Deborah's song. "In the days of Shamgar the son of Anath, in the days of Jael, the highways were unoccupied, and the travellers walked through byways. The inhabitants of the villages ceased, they ceased in Israel, until that I Deborah arose, that I arose a mother in Israel." Here's a woman who is the opposite type to Gideon. Remember his words? "My family is poor in Manasseh, and I am the least in my father's house." I'm nothing! I'm nobody! He had to be encouraged to action by God's assurance that he was not going out in his own power, but in the strength of God. Gideon is characterised by humility from first to last. But Deborah says, "In the days of Shamgar" (the man that killed six hundred Philistines with an ox-goad), "in the days of Jael" (she's the woman who put the tent-peg through the head of Sisera) — Deborah says, In the days of Shamgar and in the days of Jael things were all wrong. God's people were all in bondage. Does she infer that Shamgar and Jael didn't accomplish much? Nothing really happened in Israel until I Deborah came, I arose. How proud she is! She has not the features of Gideon at all. It's 'I' instead of what God had done.

Look at her again when you come to chapter 5 and verse 28. Many people condemn Jael for the subtle way in which she invited Sisera into her tent, assured him of his safety, gave him a bottle of milk to drink instead of water which he asked for, made him perfectly comfortable, and then stole up behind him and put a tent-peg through his temples. Do you think from verse 28 onwards of chapter 5 Deborah is very ladylike? "The mother of Sisera looked out at a window, and cried through the lattice, Why is his chariot so long in coming? why tarry the wheels of his chariots? Her wise ladies answered her, yea, she returned answer to herself, Have they not sped? have they not divided the prey; to every man a damsel or two; to Sisera a prey of divers colours, a prey of divers colours of needlework, of divers colours of needlework on both sides, meet for the necks of them that take the spoil?" Read those words over at your leisure and try to think what Deborah is doing. In a most unwomanly fashion she is mocking the grief of Sisera's mother as the old lady waits for a son who would never return from the battle. I submit that's not very ladylike, not very gentle and not very kind. I'd like to think you sisters were more tender-hearted than that.

Well, that's the type of woman that Deborah is in our chapter. And yet she has so many other commendable features — Deborah, the wife of Lapidoth. She was the wife of a flaming torch. That's what his name means — flames, lamps, splendour, torches. And the Spirit of God is pleased to tell us about this man who was the husband of Deborah. Deborah was really joined to, belonged to, was associated with, a flaming torch. I like that, don't you? A flaming torch: you think of an upheld flaming torch, radiant, light-giving.

Gideon in a later chapter goes into battle with his men with torches, yes, torches in pitchers and trumpets to blow. Yes, torches — light. 2 Corinthians chapter 4 commenting, says, "The light that shined out of the darkness." We remember that "God is light and in him is no darkness at all." And so the one who raises herself up in this chapter to be a deliverer of God's people is associated with a flaming torch — the light shining out in the darkness. Again in 2 Corinthians chapter 4 we read, "We have this treasure [of the light] in earthen vessels" and, says Paul, "God, who commanded the light to shine out of darkness, hath shined in our hearts, to give the light of the knowledge of the glory of God in the face of Jesus Christ." We have in our bodies the Spirit of God whose business it is to unfold to us the Word of God, so that we have the knowledge of the glory of God in the face of Jesus Christ. And that which we have learned from the Word of God, we have it as a light — a flaming torch — to dispel the darkness around us which has been brought in by the error that belongs to the spiritual Jabin, the god of this world, who has blinded the minds of them that believe not.

Notice please in the chapters at which we have looked, when it's the world, it is the Word of God that overcomes it; when it is the flesh, it is the Word of God that overcomes it. When it is the battle of the mind and the intellectualism of our present day trying to darken the minds of men and women, the only way to illuminate darkened minds is to be like Deborah, joined to the Word of God as a flaming torch. Take the flaming torch and hold it up on high — the light, the word — to dispel the darkness.

Now Deborah is in contact with Barak, and Barak

means lightning. And you'll notice that it says "Barak the son of Abinoam, out of Kedesh-naphtali." Naphtali means to wrestle; Kedesh means sanctuary. So here's a man whose name and location indicate "lightning out of the sanctuary of the wrestler". Lovely combination here. This woman who is linked with a flaming torch has gone to a man who is lightning, who has learned to wrestle. Lightning has to do with heaven, not earth. Why lightning? Something, as it were, in the hand of God; it belongs to the heavens. The battle we fight is not against flesh and blood but against principalities and powers, against spiritual wickednesses in the high places; and you cannot fight against them with the weapons of earth, but with the weapons that are "mighty through God". It's lightning, it's divine power, outwith the control of men, that fights against spiritual wickednesses in the heavenlies. And so you have the Word of God on earth — the flaming torch, that's the thing we use. But this woman who is associated with the flaming torch goes to a man who is a wrestler in the sanctuary, and as a result of wrestling in the sanctuary there is brought in the power of God. In fact he brings in more: "They fought from the heaven, the stars in their courses fought against Sisera." Barak is a man who wrestles in the sanctuary. He's not only associated with a woman whose husband is a flaming torch, but he moves the powers of heaven, he's operating in that sphere as well. So the Ephesian epistle says, "We wrestle not against flesh and blood, but against principalities, against powers, against the rulers of the darkness of this world, against spiritual wickedness in high places" (Ephesians 6:12).

Christians sometimes talk about wrestling with God.

Do you want to wrestle with God? Didn't Jacob wrestle with God? He did; he wrestled with a man until the break of day and he accomplished nothing. And you never will accomplish anything wrestling against God. Trying to stop God, that's what Jacob was doing, trying to overcome the angel. You remember there came a time in that night when Jacob was wrestling with the man and he couldn't prevail; the man touched his thigh and Jacob could wrestle no longer. He could neither wrestle nor run, neither fight nor flee. It was then, when he came to the end of wrestling with God, when he could only cling, that he said, "I will not let thee go until thou bless me." As long as Jacob wrestled with God there was no blessing. When he stopped wrestling and just clung, "God blessed him there." We get into the presence of God, not to wrestle against the will of God, but in the power of God to wrestle against the enemies.

Notice what the New Testament says, "We wrestle not against flesh and blood, but against principalities and powers." It's not God we wrestle against, it's God's enemies we wrestle against. When do we wrestle against principalities and powers? When we get into the sanctuary. That brings this man in, doesn't it? What was his name? Barak of Kedesh-naphtali — lightning from the sanctuary of the wrestler. This man pictures a man of the sanctuary and in the sanctuary he is praying and as a result of his praying divine power is exerted against the enemies of God's people, against principalities and powers. Not wrestling against God, but in the presence of God seeking divine power that he might be able to "stand in the evil day, and having done all, to stand."

In order to overcome Jabin and his subordinates I need to go into the sanctuary and use divine power in

6

wrestling against spiritual forces. On the earth I use the flaming torch, the Word of God, to defeat the servants of the adversary who occupy the pulpits, and who write things contradictory to the Word of God. There is something more than men behind this. There are spiritual wickednesses in the heavenlies. How can I fight them? I fight them as I get into the sanctuary. What does prayer do? When I get into God's presence and pray, I get divine power to wrestle against spiritual forces that are blinding the minds of men and women all around us today. And many of the saints are in danger of being blinded too! So I have Deborah allied to a flaming torch, and I have Barak the man who wrestles in the sanctuary. These together suggest a lovely combination. Does not John Bunyan suggest in his *Pilgrim's Progress* that there are two weapons in the Christian's armoury — "the sword of the Spirit"; and the other he invents, he calls it the weapon of "all prayer". Ephesians chapter 6 says, "Praying always with all prayer and supplications." So he has two weapons — a sword, the Word of God; and all prayer: that weapon we exert as, in the presence of God, we become recipients of divine power to wrestle against principalities and powers.

As a result of that combination please notice the lovely encouragement that Deborah gave to Barak — this is the good side of her ministry. All down the centuries among God's people spiritual Deborahs have continued this excellent ministry. For while she may not have had a very good spirit and she may have taken up a ministry that was rightly a man's, yet when she came from God with a message from God to Barak, she encouraged a weak man to do great things for God. Thank God for such sisters who stand behind and encourage men who are often failing and weak. I judge from what she says, "Hath not the Lord God of Israel commanded?" that God had already commanded Barak to go and he was such a coward that he didn't go. What a condemnation for Barak! Already told to go, but he hadn't; so a woman has to be sent to tell him to go. That would humble him! I wonder how many of us men have often been cowardly, often failed to stand up when we should have stood up, often failed God when we should have been moving. Maybe some of us look back on occasions when the Lord has used sisters to encourage us. Or maybe go a bit further as with Deborah and almost goad us; would almost rebuke and say, "Barak, hasn't the Lord already told you to go? why are you sitting there doing nothing?"

There's a man in the New Testament like that and you read about him in the last chapter of Colossians. The assembly in Colosse is told through Timothy, "Say to Archippus." Why? Because Archippus has already received a ministry that, for some reason or another, he had failed to carry out; so the assembly had to say, "Archippus, take heed to the ministry which thou hast received in the Lord, that thou fulfil it." When Barak failed to carry out the task he had been given he has the encouragement of a woman. Thank God for all sisters who, in their sphere, seek to encourage the brethren.

Turning to Deborah's song I notice (chapter 5:12) that before she says "Arise, Barak," she says "Awake, awake, Deborah," which rather indicates there was a period in her life when she was somewhat apathetic herself as to the condition of God's people, and she had to wake up. And after she wakened up she went to Barak and said, "Arise, Barak." She acknowledges she wasn't always awake: she had to wake up, then waken Barak. The result of this combined effort is (4:15), "And the Lord discomfited Sisera, and all his chariots, and all his host, with the edge of the sword;" then the end of verse 16, "And all the hosts of Sisera fell by (R.V.) the edge of the sword." It was with the sword. First of all the flaming torch as the light in the darkness; now the sword to defeat the forces of the darkness. And they are all slain with the edge of the sword.

Somebody says, "You're talking about the battle of the mind, and you said that forces who are engaged in the battle of the mind portray the devil and the principalities and powers, and we fight against them if we wrestle against them in the sanctuary. But how are we going to fight these clever academics, these clever infidels, these clever modernists, these men who make it a study to contradict the Word of God? How are we going to meet them? We are not skilled with the use of the sword, not mighty men in the Word." Well now, you sisters should be encouraging the men into battle. After all, this man was a warrior, he knew how to use the sword; and knowing how to use the sword he eventually led God's people into battle. The victory was sure. Two things come out of that. First of all, we need to know this Book (how many times shall I say that?). It's only with this Book, the sword of the Spirit, that we can meet the arguments of the clever men who oppose the Word of God. And we need among us men who are 'Baraks' who can use the sword for God.

Young men, have you it on your soul, are you willing to dedicate yourself to God, to give yourself to this Book? And are your wives willing to be like Deborah, to encourage you to spend time getting to know God's

Word? Get to know the Book first of all and then how to use it, for we need to preserve young believers from the dark influences all around us. In our outreach, in our gospel preaching, in a world that is becoming darker and darker, we need to be able to preach the fundamental principles of the Word of God. So we need spiritual Baraks, men of the sanctuary, men with a sword that they know how to use.

My dear elder brethren, we must not forget that these leaders are pictures of the elder brethren. Could you take the sword against teachers of error, agnostics, infidels or against an atheist? could you take the sword against a unitarian? do you know the Book? can you use it? You say, We're not all like that. Ah! that's it. That's why I like this bit from verse 17 onwards, and I like to link this section up with the closing verse of chapter 3, because here were two people who did not use the sword. They didn't appear to have one in any case. There is Shamgar. What sort of days did Shamgar live in? Deborah will tell you in verse 8 of chapter 5, "Was there a shield or spear seen among forty thousand in Israel?" Weapons were scarce. Remember what the Philistines did in a later day: they took away all the smiths so there wasn't a place in the whole of Israel where one could obtain a sword or get it sharpened. So Shamgar lived in a day when he didn't have a sword, and he used an ox-goad. Jael lived in a day when there were swords because all the hosts of the enemy had fallen by the edge of the sword, but she didn't have one. If she'd had, she might have been as unskilled as Peter. In Shamgar you have a farm labourer, the kind of man that would use an ox-goad. He has a pair of oxen, he's possibly drawing a plough or cart. He doesn't know

anything about war, doesn't know anything about a
sword. But he knows how to deal with the enemy — he
has an ox-goad. I don't think I would have liked to meet
Shamgar when he was advancing with his ox-goad. He
did a great work. Six hundred Philistines slain with just
an ox-goad. He knew how to use that.

Jael, she knew how to use a hammer, she knew how to
use a tent-peg; and as a nomad, possibly nearly every
night she used the hammer and tent-peg. The wind had
blown night after night, and in the rainy season the rain
had come down night after night, and she was relying on
that tent-peg to keep the tent up. It hadn't failed. She
knew she could rely on that hammer and tent-peg.
When Shamgar was facing those oxen they weren't
always placid, but he had an ox-goad. He could trust
that. And when Jael was putting up the tent she could
trust the hammer and nail.

Are any of my readers farm labourers? I mean
spiritual farm labourers. I wonder if there are any
women just like Jael. You don't know anything about
fighting, it's the last thing you want to do, but you see
you've got an enemy — Sisera — and he's got to be dealt
with. These two people are similar: Shamgar means
pilgrim and stranger; Jael was a pilgrim and stranger,
she lived in a tent, she was a nomad, moving about from
day to day. So you've got a man and a woman who were
pilgrims and strangers. Not warriors, just pilgrims and
strangers. I think of some men who have never stood on
a platform and couldn't. Sisters, of course, shouldn't
stand on the platform. However, both can join the battle
against Sisera. You say, I don't know my Bible well
enough, don't know all the arguments that are necessary
in order to enter into the battle of the mind, to be able to

prove them wrong. Shamgar was like that, he couldn't use a sword. Jael was like that, she couldn't use a sword. But they both had a part in the battle, didn't they? They both helped to deliver God's people.

How did Shamgar do it? You see, Shamgar to my mind is not a man who stands on the platform, but he's a man who looks at his Bible and says, To me it's like an ox-goad. I'm not a preacher, not a teacher, but I've proved God every day of the year in my everyday employment. Just an ox-goad, but he had proved its strength. Every time he prodded those beasts it was effective; there was never a time in his experience when that ox-goad had let him down. When a bull was getting ferocious, and possibly coming at him, he had relied on the ox-goad. Just another picture of the Word of God, but a picture of the Bible from a farm labourer's angle, not from a warrior's angle. Maybe there is somebody saying, "I could never argue with an infidel, I could never prove the Trinity, I could never prove the Deity of Christ, I could never prove the impeccability of the Lord Jesus: that isn't my job." In everyday employment you've trusted this Book and it has never let you down. You have rested on the promises of God's Word and never has it failed. That's Shamgar. He had an ox-goad that had never failed in his ordinary employment, never failed against oxen however brutal they were. And it was that appreciation of a God that never failed that he took in his hands one day and went for the Philistines, and they went down one by one, six hundred of them.

Listen my dear brother, one of the most effective ways in which you can stand against the god of this world, who has blinded the minds of them that believe not, is not by trying to argue scientifically or doctrinally or

theologically when you don't know your Bible well
enough. But if you can stand in the presence of those
who ridicule God's Word and say, "Look, it's fifty years
ago since I trusted Christ. Before I trusted Christ I was a
drunken, wicked man; but I came to Christ and trusted
him as my own Saviour and He has completely changed
my life. He has given me joy where before there was
nothing but sorrow; He has given me order and self-
control in my life where I was a violent character before;
He has made my children love me instead of hate me.
Throughout my Christian life I've read the Word of God
and rested on its promises, and after all these years I've
proved this Book is true, and I've proved its promises
never fail." That kind of argument from experience will
silence a lot of the philosophies of the atheists — just a
farm labourer's testimony to the Word of God, that the
promises in this Book are absolutely true.

You've heard of the infidel who approached a person
in the open-air meeting and mocked at the idea that the
Bible says the Lord Jesus turned water into wine, only to
find the preacher telling him that he could show him a
greater miracle. Inviting the infidel to his own home he
said he would show him how the Lord Jesus had turned
beer into furniture.

So you see just ordinary men in ordinary jobs with just
that kind of familiar knowledge of the Word of God that
brings us comfort and assurance and the promises of
God day by day. With that you can enter the battle like
Shamgar, not with a sword but with an ox-goad that
you've proved to be absolutely reliable. By saying what
the promises of God mean to you in everyday life you
can slay Philistines.

But now Jael. Every night she had come to the place

where she was going to put up her tent. And in those
days, of course, the man put up his tent and the woman
put up her tent. The man did not go into the woman's
tent, nor the woman into the man's tent; they had two
separate tents and they lived apart, these Canaanites. So
there was her tent. That's why Sisera thought he was
perfectly safe if he got inside a woman's tent; so he went
in there and hid. She was there every night, and she
would use that hammer. "It breaketh the rock in
pieces", the hammer. She took that hammer and she
took a tent-peg, she knocked those tent-pegs into the
ground, and then she went inside the tent and she slept,
and she was perfectly at peace. She knew those tent-pegs
would hold the tent up, and she would be safe, dry and
warm. Never once had those tent-pegs failed. You see,
she was just an ordinary woman with a tent-peg
experience of God. Is that the kind of knowledge you
sisters have of God? Oh! you may not be theologians,
though some of our sisters are. But suppose you are just a
poor dear married woman with children, lots to worry,
lots to harass you. You say, I've just time for a wee
prayer in the morning and maybe a verse or two, and
read a wee bit at night and pray. But you know I never
had time to study the Word of God.

My dear sister, you are a spiritual Jael. You know
God, don't you? And you trust Him in the morning
when you take the tent down for the day, and you trust
Him at night when you put the tent up. You trust the
promises of God that are like the tent-pegs around the
tent to keep it up, to keep you dry, to keep you warm, to
keep you at peace — the promises of God that never fail.
You've got a hammer — the Word of God. You've got
the tent-pegs — the promises of God. How many years

have you known the Saviour? Have you found one single occasion when the tent-pegs failed? Have any of the promises of God failed? So you are a woman like Jael with a hammer and a tent-peg. And as you "pitch your moving tent a day's march nearer home," you're sheltered by the promises of God which never fail. When an enemy of the gospel stands on your doorstep you can tell the man that years ago you trusted Christ and how you have proved the promises of God. You can give your testimony and tell how the Lord saved you. And that kind of argument could do far more than any theological argument.

You see, there is a farm labourer's appreciation of the Word of God. There is an ordinary housewife's appreciation of God's Word. And there is the practical witness of ordinary men and women relative to the faithfulness of a God. How He keeps His Word is often a more reliable argument against the darkness that is all around us than some of the clever arguments that some of us might be able to go into.

I used to live in Ipswich, England, with a grandmother who had a second-hand furniture shop. In the living room the fungus grew through the floor, and the damp went up the walls. When I was warm it was only on one side and the other side was frozen. That's the kind of home I was reared in, and as I look back I wonder how my grandmother ever made ends meet. Over the old fireplace, blackened by the smoke that constantly came out of the grate, there was a text that said, "Jehovah Jireh — The Lord will provide." When a godly old widow like that could say these words she is just pointing to one of the tent-pegs, one of the tent-pegs that never let her down.

So in the battle of the mind, it's not only the battle of the big men who know the Book and take the sword to fight. It's the battle of ordinary men who testify to the faithfulness of God and the truth of His Word. And the battle is joined by the sisters who, by their experience of the faithfulness of God in every vicissitude of life, can say, "I believe that Book because every promise in it has proved to be absolutely true."

How true it was then and is today: "For ye see your calling, brethren: how that not many wise men after the flesh, not many mighty, not many noble, are called; but God hath chosen the foolish things of the world to confound the wise, the weak things to confound the things that are mighty, the base things, the despised things, the things that are not, to bring to nought the things that are — that no flesh should glory before God." (1 Corinthians 1:26-29.)

The Lord sold Sisera into the hand of a woman: the honour of battle was Jael's and not Barak's. And so having beguiled him into her tent, she covered him, gave him milk instead of water, and stands at the door of the tent while he falls into a deep sleep. "Then Jael took a tent-peg, and took an hammer in her hand, and went softly unto him, and smote the peg into his temples, and fastened it to the ground" (v. 21) Here is the end of the man who put the battle in array for Jabin (the wisdom of this world. Notice please, Judges 5, that Sisera's mother's ladies are called "the wise ladies"). He lies dead with a nomadic woman's tent-peg hammered right through his brain. It is written, "I will destroy the wisdom of the wise" (1 Corinthians 1:19) cited from Isaiah 29:14, "Behold, I will proceed to do a marvellous work ... a marvellous work and a wonder: for the wisdom of their wise men shall perish, and the understanding of their prudent men shall be hid."

Sisera lay dead with a tent-peg through his skull! We glimpse briefly at Calvary, "the place of a skull", and view "a cross on which the Lord of glory died" and see the end of man's wisdom and the triumph of Christ the wisdom of God.

"God forbid that I should glory save in the cross of our Lord Jesus Christ" (Galatians 6:14).

Gideon — The Humble Judge

The world, the flesh and the devil, recognised as the three great enemies of God's people, have occupied our thoughts as we have considered the defeat of Chushan-rishathaim by Othniel, the subjugation of Moab and Eglon its king by Ehud, and the destruction of Jabin by Deborah, Barak and Jael. We turn now to another enemy who, sad to say, is very active among the people of God in our day; in fact, he has been active throughout the age in which we live. The divided state of the people of God is an evidence that Midian has done his work well. Midian means "strife".

Please notice that Midian was closely associated with Abraham, and therefore it is suggested that Midian is very close to all of us who through grace have become the children of Abraham through our Lord Jesus Christ. We read, "Abraham took another wife, and her name was Keturah" (Genesis 25:1). "She bare him Zimran, Jokshan, Medan, Midian, Ishbak and Shuah." Her fourth son, Midian, had five sons, and their descendants are before us in these chapters. Midian, Abraham's son, Isaac's half-brother, reminds us how close this thing called strife is to each one of us, ready to spring into action at any moment.

We should not miss the oft-repeated lesson, that when Midian crossed the border it was by divine direction. "The Lord delivered them into the hand of Midian seven years." Their coming was a divine discipline because "the children of Israel did evil in the sight of the Lord." This would suggest to us that when strife of any

93

kind breaks out in our own immediate family circle or among the Christians with whom we gather, there is a need to be exercised thereby, for it may be a discipline of God to bring us back to Himself from paths of way-wardness because, at least in heart, we have forgotten the Lord.

When Midian came in God's people lost three of their most valued possessions.

"The hand of Midian prevailed against Israel ... and the children of Israel made them the dens which are in the mountains, and caves, and strongholds" (chapter 6 verse 2).

They lost their **freedom.**

"When Israel had sown, the Midianites ... destroyed the increase of the earth" (vv. 3, 4).

They lost their **fruitfulness.**

"And left no sustenance for Israel, neither sheep, nor ox, nor ass" (v. 4).

They lost their **food.**

How true this is — when strife comes in among the people of God they lose their freedom, their fruitfulness and their food.

Have you ever had the grievous experience of being among a company of the saints when strife comes in? The beauty of Christian fellowship is marred, long-standing friendships are broken. In the place of friendship, confidence, freeness, openness, lips become silent, saints keep away from each other, suspicion grows, whispering grows, until the saints of God who should "love one another with a pure heart fervently" are "biting and devouring one another." No wonder Peter says, "See that ye love one another with a pure heart fervently ... laying aside all malice, and all guile, and hypocrisies, and envies and all evil speakings." These evils all come in, and freedom, liberty and love among the Lord's people go out when Midian, strife, comes in.

Fruitfulness is generally viewed in the Word of God as the production of the moral features of Christ in the lives of God's people. Sometimes, however, fruitfulness is viewed as blessing in the spread of the gospel and the salvation of souls. I wish to use the term in that way just now. Are you anticipating an effort in the gospel? Is there Midian-strife among the saints? I tell you, you might as well save your energy. You cannot expect blessing when strife is rife among the saints. Oh, for the need to strive together for the faith of the gospel! Let us hearken to Paul's words in that great epistle of unity in the New Testament, "I intreat thee also, true yoke-fellow, help those women which laboured with me in the gospel", that is, help them to be reconciled. Again he says, "Work out your own salvation with fear and trembling." Salvation from what? Salvation from strife, for the furtherance of the gospel is hindered when strife comes in.

Food, yes, they lost their food. Hunger was the result. Sickly saints, poverty all around, when strife came in. Is it not true that when ministry is given in an atmosphere of strife among the saints, each one is wondering if the ministry is having an effect upon saints that they do not like, hoping that a certain person is present, thinking that the word is particularly fit for them? But never for one moment thinking of taking the ministry to their own hearts and consciences. The best of ministry produces negligible results when strife comes in.

The word of God adds, "They came as grasshoppers

for multitude, for both they and their camels were
without number." Once the Midianites came in they
multiplied, and once strife comes in amongst the saints
of God it will quickly do the same. Does not James say,
"Behold how great a matter a little fire kindleth!" or
R.V., "How much wood is kindled by how small a fire!"
A great forest can be consumed by the heat of the sun on
a piece of broken glass. So strife grows. How careful we
ought to be that we do not kindle strife. It is not without
cause that the instruction is given: "The servant of the
Lord must not strive, but be gentle unto all men."

The result of this invasion was "they entered into the
land to destroy it." And Israel was brought low —
"greatly impoverished". There is nothing that will
impoverish the saints like strife. It will bring the choicest
gathering of the saints into bitterness and despondency.

This sad state of things caused God's people to cry
unto the Lord. This is the purpose of every divine
discipline in the lives of the saints — to drive us in
repentance to our knees. God graciously responds to
their cry by first of all sending unto them a prophet, a
man with a message from God to talk to them. God can
use the power of the devastating wind, the earthquake,
the flood and the fire, but His still small voice is the
vehicle His Spirit so often uses to restore His people. The
Lord, in His grace today, still uses men of God just
talking. God talks to us through men who have a
message from God. There is in Britain, particularly, no
shortage of ministry for those who wish to hear (the best
of ministry) but there is a lack of response. Let us heed
the exhortation, "Quench not the Spirit, despise not
prophesying" (1 Thessalonians 5:19, 20). This prophet
did not scold them but gently reminded them of their

history of deliverance. God had brought them up, forth and out of the hand of the Egyptians. He had driven out their enemies and given them the land. This goodness of God should have produced in them a love that would express itself in obedience. God said, "I am the Lord your God; fear not the gods of the Amorites, in whose land ye dwell." It was not unreasonable of God to expect love, obedience and fidelity after all that He had done for them. Shall we not take the challenge of this to our hearts? Does not Paul in like manner appeal to the Romans, "I beseech you therefore, brethren, by the mercies of God"? We know the words, we have enjoyed His tender mercies, but are we any better than they? Do we respond? The record says, "But ye have not obeyed my voice." The sad record of their history is alas our record too.

DEALING WITH STRIFE

Gideon is seen first in the divine record sitting under an oak when the angel of the Lord appeared to him in Ophrah. Ophrah means "dust". It says it pertained unto Joash, which means "despair". He was the Abiezrite, which means "the son of my father is help". And that's where Gideon starts. That's a good place to start, isn't it, if you want to rid God's people of strife and division, which is the outcrop of being puffed up with pride and arrogance. The man who is going to do that will need to be right down in the dust. After all, that is where the nation really was: after forty years of liberation they were now down in the dust. Gideon is down in the dust in the place of despair. Would not present conditions fill any man's heart with despair?

7

You may see a company of God's people where there is so much to be done in the gospel, and so much to be done in building up saints; and brethren and sisters are falling out about something which really doesn't matter. The people of God fall out about things that are foolish and infinitesimal. To try and reconcile saints of God when they are at strife would drive one to despair. So here's a man in the dust, and he is filled with despair.

Furthermore, he is the son of the man whose name means "my father is help". Three generations! Help is not in himself, nor in his father, but in his father's father. In other words, there was help in his grandfather's day but there was no help in his day. You know, we are often like that, aren't we? When I was a boy, and that's many years ago, they used to tell me about the great men they had fifty years before that. We are all "the son of my father is help".

In our grandfather's day — oh yes, in grandfather's day — the Spirit of God moved in the hearts of Christians and re-taught them the truth of the one body. Just over a century ago, saints of God left the denominations that divide believers into sections and give them names, because they regained the truth that believers belonged to one body. They left their denominations and gathered together to the Name of the Lord Jesus. There was hope then, for a great work was done for God. But since that day how Midian has got in among the saints, with the tragedy of all those divisions. If this had not happened there is very little doubt that that movement would have turned the world upside down. But the devil succeeded in bringing in Midian. And how many times has Midian raised his ugly head since, dividing God's people here and there, instead of there being unity among those who profess to meet in the name of the Lord Jesus?

When we think about division among God's people, strife among the people of God, could we not, all of us, get down in the dust and sit in despair? That's where Gideon sat — just there.

What was Gideon doing? I want you to notice two things. If I may follow the Revised Version here instead of the Authorized Version: "Gideon was beating out wheat in the winepress." Not by it: in it. The winepress must have been empty. It was intended for pressing grapes, not threshing barley. He has barley in the winepress — were there no grapes to press? There apparently wasn't much barley either and he was afraid of losing that: he was hiding it from the Midianites. So it was a day when there was no wine — no joy.

Gideon, he must have been a young man at this time, was beating out corn in the winepress to hide it from the Midianites. He was unconsciously preparing himself to be raised up of God to be a deliverer of God's people. He had learned that elementary lesson, which many of the dear brethren never learn, that is, to be a leader, a shepherd, a saviour, an overseer among God's people you must thresh out corn. You must know the Word of God. You cannot be a leader among God's people if you do not get down to the Word of God. Young men, if you are going to be leaders of God's people in days to come, copy Gideon. In your youth get down to the Word of God. Thresh corn, build your stock up, feed upon it, be prepared to feed others with it. You must be a thresher of corn as a qualification for being a leader among God's people.

The second lesson that Gideon must learn is, "The

angel of the Lord appeared unto him and said, The
Lord is with thee, thou mighty man of valour.'' Now, he
was anything but a mighty man. But he was reminded
first of all, "The Lord is with thee;" and the Lord being
with him is calculated to make the weakest man strong.
Said Isaiah, "Fear thou not." Why? "For I am with
thee." "Be not dismayed." Why? "For I am thy God."
Says the prophet Haggai (chapter 2), "Be strong, O
Zerubbabel; be strong, O Joshua; and be strong, all ye
people of the land, saith the Lord, and work: for I am
with you, saith the Lord of hosts." So that one of
Gideon's qualifications for what he is going to do is this:
that in himself he felt extremely weak, in himself the job
of delivering Israel from Midian was far beyond him,
and in a state of strengthlessness he would despair. But
his strength was to be made perfect in weakness, his
strength was to be conscious of his weakness: God would
pour in divine power.

You see, trying to bring the saints of God together
doesn't call for a display of natural strength. It calls for a
display of meekness. A meek man is a very strong man. A
meek man can control passion and temper. He can
control that natural tendency to speak out of place. He
can keep all his passions in check, he'll control his words,
he'll control his actions, he'll control even his looks. For
when you are trying to bring God's people together you
must not show anger, you must not speak out of place,
you must not show partisanship. You must have every
part of your being under absolute control — that's
strength. Oh no! it's not strength to give way to temper,
that's weakness. It's not strength to tell people just
exactly what you think. Moses, you remember, was the
meekest man in all the earth. For thirty-eight years he

suffered their provocations in the wilderness, and only once did he lose his temper. He was a strong man. Why? Because he had what the New Testament would call two of the fruits of the Spirit, namely self-control and meekness. How can a man become strong to destroy division and strife amongst God's people? How can he develop that self-control which is essential for that kind of work? Only as he is conscious that the Lord is with him. This will give him the strength to be a valiant man. For to bring God's people together you need strength of character. No man ever brought two striving parties together by agreeing with both. A "yes man" would agree with both. Oh no! a man who is going to bring God's people together will quietly have to say, "My dear brother, you were wrong." And just as quietly he'll say to the other brother, "Now, my brother, you were wrong." That needs great spiritual fibre. So here is a man who was naturally a retiring, quiet, perhaps somewhat shy, character afraid of the limelight. But God comes to a man like that and says, "The Lord is with thee." And because the Lord was with him he was able to do great things for God. The valour that will destroy Midianites is the valour that will bring God's people together. Oh! for men amongst us that are Gideons like that — strong when it comes to the work of reconciling saints.

Gideon is a man with an exercise and notice please, his exercise is summed up in two words: "*Why* then has all this befallen us? and *where* be all his wondrous works?" A man who is going to bring unity among God's people instead of strife will have a "why?" and a "where?". Why the present condition of things? why the lack of blessing? why the lack of liberty, of food? why?

Then he'll have a "where?". Where did the people of
God go wrong? For remember the place of reconciliation,
whether it be between God and men, or men and men, is
always the place where things went wrong. So he has an
exercise about a "why?" and a "where?".

I wonder if we have overseers like that? Humble men.
Men who despair as to their ability to bring about unity.
Men who realise they are far removed from men of God
of a past generation who could have done it. Men who
are impressed with their own weakness and inability to
grasp firmly the meekness that comes from the Spirit of
God, to be able to bring God's people together. Men
with a deep exercise to know the *why* of the present
condition, and *where* the saints of God went wrong.

God speaks to this man again and it says, "The Lord
looked upon him and said, Go in this thy might, and
thou shalt save Israel from the hand of the Midianites:
have not I sent thee?" Notice please, here is such a
transference that it's not God's might, it is Gideon's
might. It is as though God has taken His might and put
it inside Gideon, so that Gideon is now full of the might
of the Lord — "Go in this thy might." How can we go in
God's might to help His people in days of strife and
bring them together? Only in this consciousness, that
the Lord has sent us. My dear elder brother, are you
convinced, honestly in the presence of God, that you
were raised up to be an overseer? You didn't just drop
into it? you didn't just step into your father's shoes?
nobody pushed you into it? Are you really there because
the Holy Spirit raised you up and gave you a shepherd
heart? That's a real New Testament overseer. "Have
not I sent thee?" And every overseer should be
convinced before God that he has been given by God the

task of shepherding His people.

What else? "And thou shalt save Israel from the Midianites," that is, deliver them from strife. Go to the epistle in the New Testament that has to do with delivering God's people from strife; it's the lovely epistle to the Philippians where the word 'salvation' is used in diverse ways. In chapter 1, "I know that this shall turn out to my salvation through your prayers and the answering supply of the Spirit of Jesus Christ" — that's salvation from or in prison. Chapter 2, "Work out your own salvation with fear and trembling" — that's salvation from strife. Who was going to help in the matter of saving the Philippian assembly from strife? In chapter 4, the Spirit of God addresses an unnamed man and says, "I beseech thee, true yokefellow, help those women who laboured with me in the gospel" — to be reconciled. Men whom the Spirit of God has made overseers will be the men who will help these women to be reconciled and that will save the assembly from strife. Paul infers that if he were free he would come to Philippi and put his hand on the shoulders of the two women and beseech them to be reconciled, but with a chain on his wrist he couldn't come, so he says, "True yokefellow, help these women to be reconciled." A thankless task brethren, I agree, but it's your job and mine to help saints to be reconciled: because personal variance can lead to assembly strife and assembly strife can spread to catastrophic proportions.

GIDEON'S OFFERING

Gideon, impressed by the appearance of the angel of the Lord and the manifestation of grace to him, so unworthy an object, desires to bring a present and lay it before the angel. The introduction of the bringing of the present (offering, R.V.) here, is most instructive. Notice (verse 20), "Take the flesh and the unleavened cakes, and lay them upon this rock, and pour out the broth." Flesh for a burnt offering. Unleavened cakes for a meal offering. Broth poured out for a drink offering. All offered and accepted associated with a "rock" and a "rod" and a "fire". These things turn our minds to the great sacrifice of Christ — a burnt offering, a meal offering, a drink offering. And it is these aspects of His offering that are the doctrinal basis for the practical truth of Philippians 2. His complete devotedness to the will of God: "became obedient unto death, even the death of the cross" — the true Burnt Offering. That mind that was always found in the Lord Jesus: humility, no vain glory, lowliness, esteeming others better than Himself — He was the true Meal Offering. Paul in the same chapter says, "If I be poured out upon the sacrifice and service of your faith." In this he was but a faint shadow of Him "who poured out His soul unto death" — the true Drink Offering. And was He not "the Rock"? and did not Jehovah "lift up his rod"? and did not the fire devour when at the place called Calvary He offered Himself an offering and a sacrifice well-pleasing to God? This delightful Christological passage is presented to us in order that we might let this very mind be exhibited in our ways amongst the saints of God. This is the spirit that must characterise the ways of Gideon, the saviour of Israel, and must also characterise us if we would "work out the salvation of the assembly with fear and trembling."

GIDEON'S FIRST VICTORY

Before there can be deliverance for God's people and Midian be removed, the cause of the discipline must be removed. The sin of idolatry had displeased the Lord and hence he had allowed "strife" to oppress them. Before Gideon could deliver God's people from the discipline thus inflicted he must deal with this particular sin in his father's house first. This is always the way with those that God will use.

So (1) Gideon built an altar in Jehovah-shalom, "The Lord send peace". How appropriate the title and revelation of God at this time to the man raised up to promote peace among the saints. And does not the Spirit say to the Philippians saints, "the peace of God shall ..." and "the God of peace shall ..."? The Lord always reveals Himself in the way that is most suitable to His people's need.

(2) "He threw down the altar of Baal and cut down the grove that was by it." He built the altar upon this rock — was it in the very place of the sacrifice of verse 21? He used the wood of the grove for fuel to burn the sacrifice, thus showing the superiority of Jehovah to all that was associated with Baal.

(3) Gideon took ten men — an adequate witness under the Law sometimes in the O.T. Ten men represent the Law being equivalent with the expression "the ten words".

(4) He did it at night: "he feared his father's house and the men of the city." Strange mixture of faith and fear was this man. But what he did in fear, he did faithfully. It changed the course of his life and of the whole nation. John 3 tells of another man who acted at night with

similar lasting results in his life.

Gideon's father's words were bold and convincing on the coming day, "Will ye plead for Baal? will ye save him? ... Let him plead for himself, because one hath cast down his altar." Truly Gideon's boldness at night made his father bold by day. Let all who will lead God's people in days of departure remember that we must pull down the altars of Baal in our own lives before we can attempt to deliver the saints of God.

How will Gideon save Israel? Very quietly! Turn in your Bible please to chapter 6 near the end. Verse 33 says, "Then all the Midianites and the Amalekites and the children of the east were gathered together, and went over, and pitched in the valley of Jezreel." Here is God entering the battle now — the battle against strife. "But the Spirit of the Lord came upon Gideon," literally the Spirit of the Lord clothed Himself with Gideon. So was the Spirit of the Lord within Gideon, it was as though Gideon's body was just a coat the Spirit of God put on. That is what is called in the New Testament being filled with the Spirit, isn't it? Ah yes! to bring unity amongst God's people we must have men filled with the Spirit. My dear fellow overseers, do you know anything about it? You say, Do you mean we must have some kind of unusual emotion? No! you won't find that idea inside the covers of your Bible, it is not there. Then what do you mean by being filled with the Spirit? I use an old illustration, but you'll know what I mean. I move about several countries ministering God's Word, and almost invariably when I go to a house the good lady will say, "I'll show you your room," and then will add, "Make yourself at home, this is all yours as long as you are here." When in my room I open the wardrobe, and generally it's almost full with ladies' coats and dresses. I used, as a young man, to open one of the drawers of the dressing chest — well, full again. And if they had an extra piece of furniture that would be full too. You see, it was my room, I was to fill it. But I couldn't, could I? I was there alright, but I couldn't fill it because somebody else had more than filled most of it. When you trusted Christ the Spirit of God took possession of your body, but in the wardrobe you may have a lot of sin, in the dressing chest you may have a lot of self, in the tallboy you may have a lot of the world. The only way in which I could fill that room would be by the good lady removing her things. The way in which the Spirit of God will fill your life, dear brother, is when you remove all that is alien to Himself. Then you'll be filled with the Spirit. It isn't some strange emotion, some pent-up excitement. It is the most serious business of your life, when in a very solid, not emotional, way, you decide to get rid of everything and let the Spirit of God fill you. And remember there is a constant need: "Be being filled with the Spirit."

The New Testament talks about such men; it says, "Ye which are spiritual" — that's men filled with the Spirit. So the Spirit of God clothed Himself with Gideon — just about the time he was going out to meet Midian, mark you! He was going to put an end to strife amongst God's people. My New Testament says there is such a thing as "the unity of the Spirit." It never tells me I have to make it, because I couldn't: He made it. It's the unity of the Spirit. If you don't know what it is, read the opening verses of Ephesians chapter 4. What have I to do about the unity of the Spirit? It says I have to endeavour to keep the unity of the Spirit. How? Without

Midian! — in the uniting bond of peace. That gets rid of
Midian alright — the uniting bond of peace. The Spirit
of God always unites God's people. He did it on the day
of Pentecost, He has been doing it ever since.

THE FLEECE

The enemies of God's people now gather together to
fight against Israel, and we read that the Spirit of the
Lord clothed Himself with Gideon. Oh that we might
all be as he was that day, "full of the Holy Ghost and
with power." He is still however a man of fear and lack
of faith, and therefore says to God, "If thou wilt save
Israel by mine hand ..." He asks the Lord for the double
sign with the fleece of wool in the floor; and the Lord
graciously grants his request and strengthens his faith.
In making a simple application one would suggest that
the fleece represents Israel — always being fleeced,
though being the sheep of His pasture. The ground
around the fleece represents the nations. Thus Gideon
learns that God acts in sovereignty in blessing, sending
the dew of blessing on Israel and not on the nations, or
on the nations and not on Israel, according to His
sovereign will.

GATHERING GOD'S PEOPLE

What was the result of Gideon being filled with the
Spirit? Now notice this: he blew a trumpet in Abi-ezer,
i.e. a trumpet for gathering God's people together.
That's what the trumpets were for in the Old Testament
— gathering God's people together. Did you ever think
that was your task, my dear brother, gathering God's

people together? That is what Christ died for. "To gather together into one all the children of God scattered abroad." Look at verse 34, "... Abiezer was gathered together after him" (R.V.) That's good. All the saints of God where he lived were gathered together after him. Listen my brother, listen my sister too: in the local assembly where you belong does your presence tend to gather the saints together? Do you cause strife or unity? Verse 35, "And he sent messengers throughout all Manasseh; who also was gathered after him" — that's the second gathering. "And he sent messengers unto Asher, unto Zebulun, and unto Naphtali; and they came up to meet them." Abi-ezer, Manasseh, Asher, Zebulun, Naphtali — more than four tribes. Spirit-filled men will always gather God's people together. One of the reasons I think Gideon was so keen on this was because of the tribe to which he belonged. He said, "My family is the poorest in Manasseh." There was one tribe in Israel that was permanently divided; it was the tribe of Manasseh. Half of them were on one side of Jordan and the other half on the other side of Jordan; and it had been so since the days of Joshua, when certain of the tribes decided they did not want to go over Jordan. Gideon knew the tragedy of a divided tribe. Was it because he knew the tragedy of a divided tribe that he strained every muscle to get the people of God together?

I tell you, anyone who has seen division — strife among God's people with catastrophic results — will strive to bring, and keep, God's people together. So Gideon brought the saints together.

PREPARATION FOR THE BATTLE

Firstly Gideon and all the people (1) rose up early, (2) pitched beside the well of Harod ("trembling"), (3) the camp of the Midianites were on the north side of them, (4) they camped by the hill of Moreh ("instruction") in the valley of Jezreel. God is going to teach these people the lesson repeated to Zechariah in his day: "not by might, nor by power, but by my Spirit, saith the Lord" — "Lest Israel vaunt themselves against me, saying, Mine own hand hath saved me." Gideon had an army of 32,000 but God said, "The people that are with thee are too many for me to give the Midianites into thy hand." The numbers were therefore reduced to 10,000 when the fearful and trembling returned home. God said again, "The people are yet too many." Notice how the items mentioned accord with the attitude that the saints in Philippi were to adopt in seeking to destroy Midian, viz: "Work out your own salvation [from strife] with fear and trembling."

But now a further step must be taken to reduce the number still more. "Every one that lappeth of the water with his tongue, as a dog lappeth, him shalt thou set by himself; likewise every one that boweth down upon his knees to drink." It was the former group that numbered 300 who were chosen "to save you and to deliver the Midianites into thy hand." These 300, I suggest, stooped down lower "to lap" and "lapped like dogs". "Stooped lower", "took the place of dogs". Did not Mephibosheth take a similar place? "He bowed himself and said, What is thy servant, that thou shouldest look upon such a dead dog as I am?" Is not this the appropriate attitude for all to take who would seek to remove strife from amongst

God's people?

A CAKE OF BARLEY BREAD

God still would strengthen the faith of Gideon. "I have delivered the enemy's camp into thy hand. But if thou fear to go down, go thou down with Phurah thy servant ... afterwards shall thy hands be strengthened." So Gideon and Phurah went down and heard the man tell the dream of the barley bread and the interpretation his fellow put upon it: "This is nothing else save the sword of Gideon ... for into his hand hath God delivered Midian and the host." What encouragement and what instruction too. Gideon — just a barley cake, the food of the poor; so typical of Gideon, the poorest, the meanest, the least!

THE BATTLE

The three hundred men are divided into three companies of one hundred each. Was there ever such a weak army? Was there ever an army with such strange weapons? Every man had a trumpet in one hand and a pitcher and a torch in his left hand. "They brake the pitchers that were in their hands" and the light of the torches shone out. They blew with the trumpets that were in the other hand, and then cried "the sword of the Lord and of Gideon". Both hands were filled, one with a trumpet, the other with a torch — no hand left for a sword at this moment. Othniel had a sword, Ehud had a dagger, Jael had a tent-peg, Barak a sword — but here a broken vessel, a torch and a trumpet: how fitting for the teaching of this passage. You do not bring God's people together by the use of offensive weapons; beating the saints with a big stick will not unify God's people. In the battle that followed "the Lord set every man's sword against his fellow, even throughout all the host: and the host fled ... and the men of Israel gathered themselves together ..." This is surely the way to defeat Midian (strife). God's people standing together, on the one hand endeavouring to keep the unity of the Spirit in the uniting bond of peace, and God intervening on their behalf, causes Midian to destroy Midian and thus the Lord's people are delivered from strife.

Think again of Philippians chapter 2 — those opening verses that talk about relations among the saints. That they should not vaunt themselves, or be puffed up, were not to look every man on his own things, but every man also on the things of others. Down from thirty-two thousand to three hundred men. That's coming down, isn't it? And not puffing ourselves up to say, "We have done it." But in meekness coming down: that's the whole lesson of the Philippian epistle. The Lord Jesus came down — so low. Paul came down so low, Epaphroditus came down so low. Euodias and Syntyche must come down just as low if there is going to be unity among God's people. Am I getting my message over? That's the message of Gideon — coming down, getting smaller, being more humble. It is when we all learn to take the humble place and acknowledge how weak and failing we are that we shall have hope of getting peace among God's people.

One thing more, and this gives a lovely finish. "And the men of Ephraim said unto him, Why hast thou served us thus, that thou calledst us not, when thou wentest to fight with the Midianites? And they did chide with him sharply. And he said unto them, What have I done now in comparison to you? Is not the gleaning of the grapes of Ephraim better than the vintage of Abi-ezer? God hath delivered into your hands the princes of Midian, Oreb and Zeeb: and what was I able to do in comparison to you?'' (Judges 8:1-3) Here is a tribe that is angry, and angry because their importance has not been recognised among the people of God. Let us go back in their history to the time when they were entering into the land and Joshua allocated them their portion. From Joshua 17:14 we learn what was amiss with Ephraim —heady, high-minded, vaunting themselves, puffed up; they thought they were the greatest tribe in Israel. So when Gideon had succeeded in getting nearly five tribes together to destroy Midian, Ephraim was intent on trouble. You always find that, don't you? When you manage to bring the saints of God together there will always be someone wanting to start fresh trouble. So these men wanted to start more trouble. What about? Their own self-importance! "We're a great people; and why did Gideon, little insignificant Gideon, dare to gather together five tribes of God's people and destroy the Midianites and never ask us!" Do you know any saints like that? I tell you they are still alive — the Ephraimites. They are in nearly every company of God's people. So full of their own self-importance, full of their own greatness. Mind you, nobody stopped them going to help, but they didn't go. Their complaint was that they hadn't been asked. Do you know anybody like that? God blessed, and they were not in it, and they complained that they were not consulted. Someone makes a move and God blesses it, and instead of saying "Praise the Lord," they say, You shouldn't have done it

8

on your own, you should have asked us. That's the
Ephraimites. Oh, they could have gone and helped,
they really knew what was going on, but they turned a
deaf ear and then complained. And they're not dead
yet, the Ephraimites.

How do you deal with men like that if you have them
in the assembly? We will look at Jephthah later on; he
had the same problem. You'll see how two different men
dealt with the same problem. Gideon dealt with the
matter so wisely that the Ephraimites went away quite
happy. Jephthah dealt with the matter unwisely and as
a result he slew forty-two thousand men. One was a wise
man, the other a legal man. The wise man maintained
unity, and the legal man caused unparallelled strife.
Gideon knew how to deal with the situation, and poor
Jephthah didn't. What had they done? Well, they had
come in just at the end of the battle, when the thing was
just about finished. Gideon, with the help of God, had
accomplished a mighty victory, then the Ephraimites
came in just at the end and they slew the two princes of
the Midianites. Gideon says, "You did excellently: you
slew two princes. What have I done, compared with
what you have done?" They went away thinking they
had won the war, and left the saints in peace. That's a
good lesson, brethren, isn't it? If you have an awkward
brother in the assembly, well, give him the impression
he's the best, let him take the credit, and he'll be fine;
he'll be quite happy, so will the assembly. Gideon was
"not looking on his own things, but on the things of
others." He was esteeming others better than himself.

What did Jephthah do? Ephraim came and complained in a similar way and eventually Jephthah used
his sword, and forty-two thousand of his brethren were·

slain. You see, Gideon was a man of peace as an overseer. Jephthah, poor Jephthah, had good intentions but he slaughtered thousands of God's people. Overseers, to maintain peace among God's people, must be men like Gideon, men of wisdom, men of peace, men of quietness. "The servant of God must not strive." They must be willing to let that awkward brother take all the credit while they themselves do all the work. It is as simple as that.

OREB AND ZEEB

The two princes of the Midianites were slain by the men of Ephraim. Their names are significant: Oreb means "ravin", Zeeb means "wolf". How suggestive they are of those dear saints who were gripped by strife in the New Testament scriptures: "Ye bite and devour one another."

GIDEON'S TWO MISTAKES

His First Mistake

Gideon's life had been one with so many commendable features, and it had culminated in an outstanding victory giving God's people deliverance from their enemies. The people, full of enthusiasm and appreciation, immediately attribute the victory to Gideon: "Rule thou over us, both thou, and thy son, and thy son's son also: for thou hast delivered us from the hand of Midian." This is precisely what God had warned against: "Lest Israel vaunt themselves against me, saying, Mine own hand hath saved me." Had He not reduced Gideon's army to a mere three hundred men in order to prove to them that the battle was the Lord's and therefore the triumph was His? The people, however, failed to give the glory to God, failed to see the hand of their invisible Captain, and desired to make Gideon king. From the strictly worldly angle, one would ask, "What better king could they possibly have?" But it was not yet God's time for a king. He would one day in His own time bring in David, but it was not yet God's time to establish a dynasty of kings in the midst of His people. Said Gideon, "I will not rule over you, neither shall my son rule over you: the LORD shall rule over you." The nation wanted to be like the nations and have a visible king who would lead them in battle. They had the best possible form of rule. God was their King — all-knowing, all-wise and all-powerful. No earthly king could compare with Him. But flesh must have someone visible, tangible, like to themselves; so they were already rejecting God's rule by desiring Gideon to rule over them. They also desired to establish a succession. Human reason would consider this to be far superior to God's way. God's way was so haphazard — they did not know who the next judge would be, or where to find him. They often had to wait a number of years between the death of one judge and the raising up of another, and in that interval between each judge they always suffered defeat and endured bondage — God's way had not worked! Why not have a recognised king, and establish a succession of kings in a family — a dynasty? That would be so much better than God's way! Gideon recognised, however, like the parents of Elimelech, "My God is King!" Gideon had seventy sons, doubtless like Gideon's brethren "each one resembled the child of a king."

While Gideon recognised the rule of God and therefore refused to become king, the vanity of his heart caused him to desire the office of priesthood. God had a priesthood at this time and the tabernacle was in Shiloh, and to that priesthood and sanctuary the people should have gone. But Gideon would in miniature set up his own priesthood. His vain heart might have reasoned that his experience fitted him for that office. Had not the angel of the Lord appeared to him? had he not offered sacrifices which had been accepted? had God not on so many occasions spoken to him, and through him had given victory to the people? He would ask the people to bring the golden ear-rings — 1700 shekels of gold — besides crescents and pendants and purple raiment that were on the kings of Midian and the chains that were round the camels' necks. What vanity! A man who, being of the tribe of Manasseh, could never be a priest, desires that the people bring him this colossal wealth to make an ephod (far more elaborate and valuable than the ephod of the tabernacle), that he might put it in his city in Ophrah. He no doubt intended that the people might come to him, that through this ephod he might be a mediator between them and God. Notice what God says about it: "All Israel went a-whoring after it, which thing became a snare unto Gideon." A-whoring — this was considered by the God of heaven spiritual adultery. Was not God their God? should their affection not be toward Him? had He not His tabernacle, His priesthood? was there not an ephod in Shiloh? To come through another way, another priesthood, in anther place, is to Jehovah whoredom. The hearts of the people went out toward the ephod instead of the Lord himself.

What tragic results followed — it became a snare to Gideon. But sadder still, we read in verse 33, "When Gideon was dead, the children of Israel turned again, and went a-whoring after Baalim, and made Baal-berith their god." What an easy step between a-whoring after the valuable, gold, idol-like ephod in Ophrah, and going a-whoring after Baalim and Baal-berith. Gideon had thus paved the way for that turning back to idolatry by the introduction of his ephod. His first victory was to destroy the altar of Baal and cut down the grove and thus deliver from idolatry. When he was old, by his ephod he led the people back into idolatry. How important for each of us to learn that by lack of discernment and watchfulness we may, when we are old, undo the work we have been enabled to do for God when we were young.

His Second Mistake

When he became older, his battles fought and peace established, living in Ophrah, judging God's people for forty years, we read "He dwelt in his own house. And Gideon had seventy sons of his body begotten: for he had many wives." Thus when days of business for God were over and quietness was in the land, he seems to have spent his time over-indulging the flesh. Not content with many wives, he has a concubine in Shechem. Did not outlandish women cause Solomon to sin? What shall be said of this concubine? Of her he had a son, outwith the bonds of holy wedlock, and when he was born Gideon denied his former convictions. Had he not said, "I will not reign over you"? But now, though he had seventy sons whom he would not make king ("neither shall my sons reign over you"), he names this illegitimate son of the flesh Abimelech, "my father is king". He was indeed the least worthy to bear such a name, had it even been true.

What a tragic end to such a noble life! Mistake number one brought back idolatry. Mistake number two brought in a son of the flesh who destroyed Gideon's seventy sons and brought in strife, treachery and civil war among the people. What a sad end! It is indeed good to start well, better to go on well, better still to finish well. May the Lord help us so to do.

Abimelech — The Carnal Judge

Abimelech reigned. The word of God says he was prince over Israel and he bore the title of king for three years. We have before us the first king in Israel; it wasn't Saul, but Abimelech. But he was only king of a small area of the country.

In the previous chapter we were looking at the two colossal mistakes that Gideon made at the end of a lovely life. We noticed that as a young man he had destroyed the idols and cut down the grove. In other words he commenced to deliver God's people from the particular sin of that time: the sin of idolatry. When he was old he conceived the idea of becoming a priest in the midst of God's people and so he made an ephod. A valuable ephod, it looked exactly like an idol and was worth lots of money. Having put it in his own city, all the people came to it and to Gideon in order to enquire of God. The Word of God says, "All Israel went a-whoring after it." When Gideon was dead the people quickly changed that ephod for an idol of Baal, and so the man who had been raised up to deliver the people from Baal-worship, before he died, made an ephod that led the people back to Baal-worship.

Again, Gideon was raised up of God to deliver His people from Midian which, we saw, was strife. But not only had he begotten seventy sons of his own body, he had a concubine in Shechem of whom was born Abimelech, whose name means "my father is king". Abimelech brought strife throughout the nation, until Abimelech destroyed the men of Shechem and the men

120

of Shechem destroyed Abimelech. The man who was raised up to deliver God's people from strife, laid the seeds of strife by his indulgence of the flesh in his later years. What a solemn lesson for all of us, those of us particularly who are getting older. It is possible that when we were young we stood for God, maybe sometimes somewhat unwisely with the rashness of youth, but oh! the danger when we are old of undoing completely the good which we did in our early years.

When we were young we endeavoured to lead God's people out of Christendom. When we are old we could lead them back into Christendom. When we were young we looked upon the world as an abhorrent thing. When we are old we could allow the world into our hearts, negativing in later years all we stood for in our youth. Younger men and women, it is good to see you starting well, and excellent to see the large number of young people now in the assemblies in this country. My dear young Christian, it is an excellent thing to start well, it is better to go on well, and better still to finish well. Gideon started well, went on well, but made two mistakes that were catastrophic. If Gideon had not made those two mistakes, chapter 9 of Judges couldn't have been written.

Before leaving chapter 8 let us note that God's people should have been so grateful to Gideon for all the things he had done. He had accomplished for them, under the hand of God, a wondrous deliverance, and kept them in peace for forty years. Yet we read, "And the children of Israel remembered not the Lord their God, who had delivered them out of the hands of all their enemies on every side; neither showed they kindness to the house of Jerubbaal, namely Gideon." How soon God's people forget godly leaders and turn away from the things they taught! It seems as though the Spirit of God would tell us that they owed a debt, not only to Gideon, but to his seventy sons. But they forgot Gideon and they showed no kindness to the sons of the man who had been such a wonderful leader.

We live in days when men and women are absolutely ungrateful, unthankful for all the benefits that God has bestowed upon them. That spirit comes in among the people of God! We should be grateful to the man or the woman who led us to Christ. Said Paul, "I say not unto thee how thou owest to me thine own self besides." He's impressing Philemon with the debt of gratitude he owes because he had led him to Christ. In Romans chapter 16, Paul is impressing upon the saints the debt they owe to Priscilla and Aquila and he says, "Unto whom not only I give thanks but also all the churches of the Gentiles." The last chapter of the Hebrew epistle tells us to remember them that were our guides, that is, the overseers who have passed away. This chapter goes a step further and shows that God seems to expect that kindness would be shown to the sons of the man who had been such an excellent leader among His people.

"And Abimelech the son of Jerubbaal went to Shechem unto his mother's brethren." You'll notice that Abimelech had a father, Gideon; but he also had a mother. His father had seventy sons; his mother had brethren. Notice where Abimelech's affinity was. Who was he linked with? He is a son of the flesh, a carnal man, he only has carnal instincts. He has seventy brothers, all men like Gideon, all, if you like, spiritual men. But he has no oneness with spiritual men. On the other hand this carnal man has his mother's brethren, and he has the family of the house of his mother's father. He says, "I am your flesh" — there was a carnal connection. Gideon's seventy sons had doubtless been reared in his home, under his roof, in his city. This carnal man, it appears, had been reared separately. A carnal man, with a carnal mother, with carnal relatives, in carnal circumstances. This man is going to become a ruler, a judge, a king of God's people; and we said before that the judges in the Book of Judges are a picture of overseeing brethren. Do you think there have ever been carnal men as overseers in assemblies of God's people? In the New Testament I see what overseers should be like. I am very conscious that many overseers in the assemblies of God's people are not what 1 Timothy chapter 3 says they should be. We are viewing the subject not from the angle of what should be but from what actually is: that is different. All of us know who have had any experience among the people of God that there are spiritual overseers and there are carnal overseers. The first question they ought to ask themselves is, "Am I spiritual or am I carnal?" Now, what do spiritual men do? They keep company with spiritual men and women. The New Testament says they sing spiritual songs and they use spiritual language and they worship God in the Spirit. Spiritual men, says 1 Corinthians chapter 14, will acknowledge that what Paul wrote in his epistles is the commandment of the Lord.

What are carnal or fleshly men? All of us know that there is about us that thing called flesh. And a carnal man thinks in a fleshly way, he talks in a fleshly way, acts in a fleshly way, and he likes fleshly companions. My dear brother, my dear sister, what are you, what am I?

I'm not asking you if you are in assembly fellowship, I'm taking that for granted. I'm asking you, are you carnal or spiritual? For every company of God's people has some folks that are carnal and some that are spiritual. Galatians says, "Ye which are spiritual restore such an one." That shows there were men in the Galatian assemblies who honestly before God could say, "Yes, I'm spiritual." They weren't proud men, because they were told to do things in a spirit of meekness, trembling with fear. But they were spiritual. And it was spiritual men who had to restore the one who had been overtaken in a fault. In other words the shepherds among God's people should be spiritual men.

It's a sad thing that this man who was carnal and who took the leadership among God's people was a son of Gideon. What does that mean for our consciences? Simply this. My dear brother, the fact that your father was spiritual doesn't mean that you are spiritual. My dear sister, the fact that your mother was spiritual doesn't mean that you are spiritual. Gideon was a man of whom it was said on one occasion, "The Spirit of God clothed himself with Gideon." What a spiritual man! But he had a son who was so carnal you couldn't even tell whether he was saved or not. He never mentions the name of the Lord. Have you ever known spiritual men to have carnal sons? Have you ever known spiritual women to have carnal daughters? Father and mother breathing the atmosphere of heaven; their offspring acting carnally, speaking carnally, thinking carnally, weighing up every situation the way a worldling would weigh it up, with worldly wisdom, with business acumen — that's carnal — not judging things by spiritual means according to the Word of God. This carnal man says to himself, "My father's dead. I'd like to rule God's people." What a tragedy when a carnal man wants to become an overseer among God's people! Oh, I know a carnal man can't be a real overseer because the Word of God says, "In the which the Holy Ghost hath made you overseers," and the Holy Ghost does not raise up carnal men to be overseers; but in many assemblies you may have carnal men that take the place of overseers.

There is something about the flesh in Abimelech that says, "I want to be king." Carnal men often like to force themselves forward in the things of God, take a place of prominence, a place of leadership. Maybe things haven't been done according to their way of thinking in the assembly and they say, "Now that brother so-and-so is dead if I can get in there I'll turn the assembly around the way I want it." Maybe saying, "Those old brethren are old-fashioned, antiquated, they are not with it. If I can get the reins I'll alter things." That's carnality. Are any of my readers like that? Maybe you thought you would just get in among the overseeing brethren and dominate the situation and then you could bring in your carnal ideas. Or maybe you are waiting until some saintly old brother is dead and then it will be your opportunity to get in and bring in ideas entirely different from what has been practised in the assembly before. That's carnality.

You say, But surely that doesn't happen! Then what was Paul talking about in Acts chapter 20 when he said, "Grievous wolves shall enter in," and "Of your own selves shall men arise"? What was Peter talking about when he saw the danger of "lording it over God's heritage"? And what was Diotrephes, if he wasn't a carnal man? You are told in the context of Diotrephes not to follow that which is evil but that which is good. I judge the evil is found in Diotrephes and the good in Demetrius. When the Spirit of God uses the word 'evil' against Diotrephes it puts the question immediately into our minds, Was the man saved or not? He was in the assembly, he was an overseer, and he absolutely dominated the assembly, even "casting the brethren out of the church."

Could there be overseers like that today, so carnal that you wonder if they are saved? They don't even seem to talk the language of the people of God nor enter into spiritual things. Oh! they are excellent organisers, run the assembly almost like a board of directors, every oversight meeting like a business A.G.M. But when it comes to the Word of God and the spiritual assessment of the situation and spiritual guidance for the assembly, they are sadly lacking. Carnal men. Have you met those men among the people of God? They can talk to you about business, about the world, about property, and everything like that. Say something about the Scriptures and they become silent. They are not in that realm at all. And yet, like Abimelech, that kind of man would like to be a leader amongst God's people.

Let us examine the chapter. A carnal man wants to be a leader among God's people. His father Gideon had rejected the idea of being king; but Abimelech is one, with several others, that wanted to bring in kingship before God's time. Abimelech wanted to be king. Jephthah had a daughter; Eli had appointed his sons to be judges; and Samuel made the same mistake of appointing his sons to be judges. This desire to be king is the thing that appeals to carnality. Paul says, "Of your own selves shall men arise." Somebody up above the overseers, Diotrephes — a king. You know perfectly well from the New Testament scriptures that God does not approve of one king in the local assembly. He doesn't even have one bishop or one elder. Rule in God's assembly is a plurality. So this idea of dominance, of a king, is foreign both to this period of the Old Testament and to the New Testament scriptures. But Abimelech wanted to be absolute ruler among God's people. There are men in the companies of God's people today, and even though they acknowledge that the New Testament talks of a plurality of overseers, yet in that circle of overseers they want to be dominant, want their own way, want to rule, want to be everything; and men that do that are showing the features of carnal men.

Abimelech, in order to obtain for himself the position of king, goes to his mother's brethren, the house of his mother's father. In other words he goes to those to whom he can say, "I am your brother, ye are my brethren." He makes a carnal approach to carnal men and says, "Speak, I pray you, in the ears of the men of Shechem." What does that mean for our instruction? Well, if you get a dominant, carnal man who wants to alter things in the assembly and get things done his own way, he will contact the carnal folk in the meeting and gather a party of men and women around him who will back him up in his carnal ideas. You understand what I mean, don't you? Have you ever heard of parties, a little group in an assembly agitating for a certain line of things that is going to alter what has been the practice before? At the head of them you have a powerful man and the rest backing him up — Abimelech and his carnal associates.

When there is a carnal man in the assembly who wants to take over where spirituality has reigned before, he will always seek the backing of carnal men and women. Sometimes as I move round the assemblies I hear of things like this. A man who wants to change things and he'll say, "If you go around the assembly there are a lot of folk that agree with what I say." Men who are trying to get the leadership, who are carnal, will always get the support of carnal brethren and sisters. So Abimelech approached his mother's brethren and the brethren of his mother's father, and suggested that they did a wee bit of "lobbying". Just go round the men of Shechem and whisper in their ears, "Wouldn't it be better for you to have one man reigning over you than the seventy sons of Gideon to reign over you? Wouldn't it be easier for one man to rule than seventy men to rule? And after all, I am your brother." So there is, first of all, Abimelech. Then he gets the support of carnal relatives. And then he spreads the leaven, shall we say, of his dissatisfaction with the sons of Gideon to the company. What is he appealing to? He says, "I'm one of your brothers, my mother was a Shechemite. She was not of Gideon's family — she married him, but she was a Shechemite. And so I'm one of your brethren. I'm one with you!"

My dear young brother and sister, never follow a splinter group in an assembly. Never listen to those stories of dissatisfaction with what the overseers are doing that circulate among the saints. Never lend your ear to those who would tell you that the overseeing brethren are out of date and old-fashioned and there needs to be an alteration here or there. For if you lend your ear to that, you will become like the people of Shechem that listened to the brethren of Abimelech. Here he is bringing together a following that is going to destroy the sons of Gideon and establish himself as a leader among God's people. Watch the carnal man who seeks to get support from carnal men and women, and watch him as he moves among God's people trying to create dissatisfaction. As a result of his efforts Abimelech eventually gets a large following. Let me say this: the people who, like Abimelech, cause trouble among God's people often boast of having a far bigger following than they really have.

Let us now observe that when they listen to what he has to say and are impressed by it, "they gave him threescore and ten pieces of silver out of the house of Baal-berith, wherewith Abimelech hired vain and light persons" to slay his brethren. How many brethren did they slay? Seventy. How much money did they give him to hire vain and lewd persons? Seventy pieces of silver. In other words, his assessment and their assessment of the value of the sons of Gideon was that they were worth one silver piece each. They reckoned Joseph was worth twenty. Our Lord Jesus Christ was sold for thirty — the price of a slave. But the sons of Gideon — one silver piece each. That is the way carnal men assess spiritual men. That is carnality assessing spirituality. They say, "You know, the overseeing brethren in our meeting are not worth ten cents, not worth anything, almost valueless." Seventy pieces of silver, one little piece of silver for the life of one man.

My dear brother, I want to ask you, What is your assessment of spiritual men and women? do you say they are old-fashioned, that they are not with it? do you push them on one side? I ask you, What value do you put on spiritual men and women? At a conference recently in England one of the speakers dared to say that the

9

overseers of the assemblies were like geriatric generals.
Another mocked at "little men with big Bibles"; in other
words, that was his opinion of spiritual overseers. In
these days of worldly thinking and carnality, would you
push spirituality on one side and say they are not worth
anything? That's what Abimelech would do with these
men, worth only one silver piece each. Does not the New
Testament say, "Hold them in double honour"? which
means at the very least that you give spiritual men
double respect and recognize that men whom God has
raised up to be leaders among His people have to be
revered.

Abimelech was not beyond using those seventy pieces
of silver to hire vain and light persons. Vain means
empty and worthless; light means rash or wanton. So he
hired worthless wanton men in order to do his foul work
of slaying seventy spiritual men. Often the 'Abimelechs'
among God's people are cunning men. They try to
influence simple folk to further their cause, while they
often keep in the background. Now, I'm not saying that
those dear simple men and women are vain and lewd
and wanton, but cunning Abimelechs use them. You
can almost hear the echo of the other man's voice in the
background, and you say to yourself, That didn't come
from that brother at all, that comes from so-and-so, the
Abimelech in the background.

Having moved in the background and obtained a
following, he now buys people among the vain and light
persons to do his dirty work. You say, Can people be
bought among God's people? You've never heard of a
person in an assembly yet who went along to a brother
or sister and said, If I pay you so much will you further
my cause? That wouldn't happen. But there are other

ways by which the people of God can be influenced to
follow men that cause strife and party faction among
God's people. You can bestow favours. You can be so
kind that a brother or sister will feel almost obligated to
support your cause. You can possibly, on some occasion,
lavish something upon them that is so unexpected that
you put them into lasting debt to yourself. Men that
want to be Abimelechs among God's people often act in
this way. They have folks obligated to them for some
kindness that they have shown, and they think they can
rely upon them to back them up in the schemes they
have planned or the things they want to do. It's a good
thing to be able to walk among the people of God
without being under obligation to anybody, as one of
the Lord's free men.

Having hired these vain and light persons which
followed him, "Abimelech went unto his father's house
at Ophrah, and slew his brethren the sons of Jerubbaal,
being threescore and ten persons, upon one stone." That
is rather an interesting expression: "he slew them upon
one stone." It must have been a kind of ceremonial
slaying. It must have been a one-by-one execution. And
how did these wanton men manage to do that? I think
there must have been far more than seventy of them —
possibly a great crowd of them — otherwise how could
they have lined up the seventy sons of Gideon and
executed them one by one, all upon one stone? How did
Abimelech die? With one stone on his head! A woman,
from the top of the tower, dropped a stone on his head
and broke his skull. That is the poetic discipline of God,
that the man who dared to slay seventy spiritual men
upon one stone, died in shame with a woman dropping
one stone upon his head. That is God's answer to what

he did! The New Testament says "If any man defile the temple of God, him will God destroy" (1 Corinthians 3:17). And also "Whatsoever a man soweth, that shall he also reap" (Galatians 6:7). In other words, God will poetically answer the Abimelechs among His people. Those who ruthlessly destroy will be destroyed by God. Now, what did he do? This man hired these wanton wasteful creatures to slay seventy spiritual men. Who was responsible? Abimelech, the carnal man, for slaying seventy men.

There are assemblies of God's people today where godly elders, spiritual men, have been pushed on one side. And in their place sit worldly men with worldly ideas, with no intention of obeying the Word of God, and they run the assembly just as though they were running a business company. Slaying spiritual men, pushing them on one side, so that as carnal Abimelechs they could reign as kings and say, "Now make me king." Always watch the man who tries to push himself into oversight work, watch the man who is wanting to dominate the assembly.

So the Word says, "All the men of Shechem gathered together, and all the house of Millo, and went, and made Abimelech king, by the oak of the pillar that was in Shechem." You will notice that God raised up Othniel; God raised up Ehud; the angel of the Lord appeared unto Gideon. But here the people gathered together and made Abimelech king. Is that what we do in the assemblies of God's people? does the assembly gather together to make certain men overseers? do you vote the overseers into position by common ballot, or by a show of hands? are they in the place they occupy because of their popularity in the assembly? Or is the

New Testament right when it says, "In the which the Holy Ghost hath made you overseers"? What kind of people then do you think will be the leaders of God's people, if the majority of the assembly are carnal and they choose their overseers? will they not choose carnal men? It is the Holy Spirit that makes overseers.

How then do you recognize overseers in the local assembly? If a man desire the work of an overseer, says the New Testament scriptures, he must first of all have certain moral qualities, and these are absolutely basic and essential for being an overseer. But then according to the last chapter of John's Gospel, if a man is going to shepherd God's people he must be characterised by love for Christ, he must be characterised by a love for the flock. So that if the Holy Ghost raises up overseers they will be of certain moral character. Then they will be men that show a very great love for Christ, and a great love for the Lord's people because of their love for Christ. The epistle to the Corinthians says that there were certain people that addicted themselves (they made it the central dominating passion of their lives) to the work of the Lord. So when the Holy Ghost raises up overseers they will be men of moral character; not Abimelechs. They will be men that love the Lord, not themselves. Men that love the Lord's people and sacrifice themselves. And they will addict their whole lives to a passionate care of the people of God. They will be men entirely different from Abimelech.

JOTHAM'S PARABLE

The rather interesting parable told by Jotham must be interpreted in the context, of course, of a man of

Abimelech character becoming ruler over God's people instead of choice characters like, shall we say, the seventy sons of Gideon. There are three kinds of trees here, and they represent men found among the people of God. And so we are going to see "men, as trees walking." The trees went forth of a time, said Jotham, to anoint a king over them, and approached the olive-tree, then the fig-tree, and then the vine. Here are three trees among all the trees of the forest which, in the Word of God, are looked upon as ideal trees. These three are used relative to the nation of Israel, though they are not used in that context in this chapter. Using the three trees relative to Israel, you have the olive as the nation of Israel in testimony, the fig-tree as the nation of Israel politically, and the vine as the nation of Israel bringing forth pleasure for the palate of God. We conclude then that these three trees are used in the Word of God to symbolize that which is good and pleasing to God.

First of all the olive-tree. And it is evident that wherever you have the olive-tree you are thinking of things pertaining to the Spirit of God. So many times in tabernacle scenes and in temple scenes you have the oil that is put upon, mingled with, etc., and each time the oil speaks of the Spirit of God. This tree is brought before us as the one that produces fatness — richness, prosperity, if you like — "wherewith by me they honour God and man." And so we shall consider an olive-tree man in an assembly.

An olive-tree man is a Spirit-filled man, a man who spiritually is fat and prosperous. "The olive-tree by which they honour God." The oil that honours God suggests a man who can touch holy things, can minister, if you like, in the sanctuary. For we worship by the Spirit of God. You can recognize in the assembly, can you not, a spiritual man, and a man who is prospering in the things of God? He's a man, too, who on a Lord's day morning, especially, can lead the saints of God right into the sanctuary. He can touch the throne. It's as though the Spirit of God uses him as a vehicle to bring before the saints the wonder of the excellency of Christ. The Spirit bringing to us the things of Christ, showing them to us in order that we speak well of Him to God.

Then we think again of the oil that honours man, and are reminded of the good Samaritan, pouring in oil and wine to the man on the Jericho road — a man full of the fruit of the Spirit, a lovely man. If you have a man like that in your assembly, you have a man for which to thank God.

Would you go to that man and say, "We're needing a king in our assembly, someone just to be a figure-head, someone to be the chairman of things and take the place of domination"? We are living in a day when some of the companies of God's people are saying, "We need a pastor. We are not satisfied any more with the scriptural pattern of overseeing brethren. At least we must have a co-ordinator to co-ordinate all the activities of the assembly." If you have an 'olive-tree man' in the assembly and say to him, "We want an official leader, we want to be like the denominations around us," he'll say to you, "Should I leave my prosperity wherewith by me they honour God and man, and go just to be a figure-head waving over the rest of my brethren?" Do you think that man would do that? Why, if he is a man who can judge himself aright in the presence of God and judge the need of the saints, he will say to you, "I feel what the assembly needs from me is my Spirit-given ministry. I wouldn't like to have to give that up just to be a king. For after all being a king is just being a figure-head." So men who are olive men in the assembly know that God has given to them a place, a very useful place, the place for which Christ has fitted them, ministering to God and ministering to the saints in the power of the Spirit of God. Men like that don't want to be kings in the assembly!

In the assembly where I have fellowship we have several men among our overseeing brethren of that character. I have never found that one of them wanted to lift himself up above the rest of the brethren and say, Look here, in future I'm going to be the pastor here. No! these dear men who are fitted like that just go quietly about among the assembly, their spiritual touch helping all the saints, their prosperity not only seen in the meetings, but with a wee word here and there, spiritually refreshing the saints. Ah yes, they have a ministry, a ministry that helps the assembly. On Lord's day morning you'll get these dear men rising and taking you right into the sanctuary, and you'll see the same men out at the open-air meeting and giving out tracts. My word! they've got plenty to do. None of them has time to give up being spiritual in order to be a king. None of them has time to stop prospering, by reading the Word of God, to go and be a king. None of them has time to stop leading the saints in worship to go and be a king. Nor have they time to stop gospel work to go and be a king. A king seems to be an idle job, doesn't it? Just waving over the saints. Just happy to say, I'm the big chief here; I'm really king; everybody bows to me here. That's all there is in it —"waving to and fro over the trees."

Let us consider the next man. "The fig-tree said unto them, Shall I forsake my sweetness, and my good fruit, to go and wave to and fro over the trees?" A fig-tree is characterised by two things — sweetness and goodness. Are there any men like that in the assembly — sweet and good? They are scarce. I don't know if this man is particularly gifted, if he has a gift that would bring him to the platform. You wouldn't necessarily ask him to preach the gospel or to minister the Word. But oh! isn't he sweet and good? As he moves among the saints of God he brings with him the very sweetness of Christ, and you know how sweet the Lord is, don't you? There are men among us who carry something of the very sweetness of Christ. They spend a long while in His presence. Not only can they talk about Him until you can almost see Him, but when you look at their lives you see the humility of Christ, the grace of Christ, the uprightness of Christ, the genuineness of Christ. In your hearts all you have learned to appreciate of the loveliness of Christ: you see some of that in fig-tree men as they move among the people of God.

My dear brother, maybe some of us would like to think we are spiritual men. I wonder if we could ask ourselves, as elder brethren, the question, Am I a sweet man? am I a good man? You generally associate sweetness with sisters, you think of all their tender graces that us men so often lack. I am not suggesting for a moment that our Lord Jesus was in any way effeminate, for He was doubtless a man of perfect physique, perfect strength; yet when you look at the perfect humanity of Christ you see a touch that is more tender than a mother's, a sympathy that truly passes the love of women. The Lord Jesus groaned in the presence of

death, tears poured down His face. He heaved a sigh
when a man had an impediment in his speech and was
deaf too. He looked at a city, and not merely wept tears
but lifted up His voice and cried audibly — a thing men
rarely do. The sweetness, the tenderness, the humility,
the grace of Christ. That is a true shepherd heart. That
is the way true shepherds care. They show such a
tenderness. What does it say of the Saviour? "He carries
the lambs in His bosom." Are we overseers like that —
sweet and good? Does the assembly know we are good?
Do sinners around know we are good? We have become
so used to preaching in the gospel that salvation is not of
works, that we have forgotten that one of the things that
accompanies salvation is good works. We, as individuals,
should be characterised by good works — not to be
saved, but because we are saved. Assemblies should be
characterised by good works. Elders should be men
given to hospitality, sweet and good. I'm sure if you have
a man like that in your local assembly he is not wanting
to be chief, because he is humble, he is kind, and he will
stoop down to people's feet and will serve them. He's not
wanting a higher place. He is hunting for a lower place.
So the fig tree says, "You are wanting me to leave my
humble, sweet, kind service that the saints of God so
much need. You want me to leave that and just go to
wave over the cedars. No! No!"

Consider the third man, the vine. "The vine said unto
them, Should I leave my wine, which cheereth God and
man?" That's lovely, isn't it? A vine man can cheer the
heart of God and he can cheer the heart of man. I
suppose there is nothing cheers the heart of God more
than men appreciating His blessed Son. Have you
noticed that the Saviour says "I am the true vine"? Most

of the saints think so much about the branches that they forget the original statement, "I am the true vine. My Father is the husbandman." From that true vine there are pressed to the lips of God the most luscious grapes. Where do they come from? Well, the One who is the true vine. The true vine, what Israel failed to be, what we fail to a large extent to be, Christ was; and the lips of God that were longing for sweet refreshment found it all in Christ, as the lovely sweetness of Christ was pressed to the palate of Jehovah — Christ bringing pleasure to God. This vine man in the assembly, he can refresh the lips of God with Christ. He can bring God joy. He can bring Christ to the lips of the saints so that their needs are met. Here is a man who can express to God and to men the loveliness of Christ.

It is true that if you have three men like that in your local assembly you have three overseers for which to thank God. And they are real overseers. What do they do? They refresh God and man. They bring sweetness and kindness and rest and care. They feed the saints with Christ, and bring God pleasure. They are real overseers: none of them will want to leave the work that they are doing in order to be king. So among the overseeing brethren there are the three of them, just trees among trees, working together. They are doing the job that God has fitted them for, they are meeting the needs of God and men in their respective spheres, none of them thinking about being king. If you have overseeing brethren that work harmoniously together like that, you'll have a happy assembly.

There is, however, in this particular chapter, another brother. His name is Mr. Bramble. He is just a thornbush. To him they say, "Come thou and reign over us."

Whoever would think of making a black, dirty, prickly old bramble king? Well of course not, but who would have thought of making a man like Abimelech king over God's people? And who would have thought of having a man like Diotrephes as an elder in an assembly? But Abimelech is there in Judges chapter 9, and is he not a thorn-bush? Diotrephes is there in 3rd John. Some assemblies, sadly enough, have men of that character — thorn-bushes — and sometimes they get in among the overseeing brethren and want to wave over the top of the trees. You'll have the fig-tree brother, the olive-tree brother and the vine-tree brother there, and they will all be doing their jobs. But the bramble-bush brother, the thorn-bush, he says "I'll be king."

I wonder if you're acquainted with a bramble or thorn-bush brother? I know many of them — real thorn-bushes. A thorn-bush brother never needs to be persuaded to become chief. In fact, a thorn-bush brother is like Abimelech: he can't wait. He'll go to the overseeing brethren and say, "It's strange you brethren haven't recognized before that I'm an overseer." Have you ever met anybody like that? They suggest themselves to be overseers. Oh no! they wouldn't believe in voting overseers in, but they don't mind suggesting themselves. They will often say, "I don't meet with the recognised elders in the assembly. I don't accept any of them as overseers. But I'm an overseer."

Let us look at what a thorn-bush brother is like. "Then said all the trees unto the thorn-bush, Come thou and reign over us." You don't read that, with mock humility, the bramble-bush looked sheepish and said, "No, I don't think you should ask me to do that." This bramble-bush didn't even pretend mock humility and didn't try to suggest this was a job beyond him altogether. He said, "If in truth ye anoint me king over you, then come and put your trust in my shadow." Ever heard anything so ridiculous? A thorn-bush — hardly has the strength to get above the ground! There it is, surrounded by cedars, and it is so near the ground it can hardly get a speck of sunlight on it; it's under the shadow of the other trees. Yet a thorn says, Come and get under my shadow. But really it was so low, so strengthless, so near the ground, it needed the protection of all the other trees. Thorn-bush brethren are like that. They don't realise that they need the cheer of the vine, the goodness and sweetness of the fig-tree, the oil of the olive; and they certainly need the protection of those cedars. They do not think they need their fellow brethren and sisters at all! They are quite confident of themselves. They are those self-opinionated brethren who think they are perfectly competent to do everything, and everybody else in the assembly is incompetent. The bramble-bush would look up at those lordly cedars, but he has the audacity to say, Come and put your trust in my shadow. Have you ever tried to get under the shadow of a thorn-bush? I should imagine that you would get a thorn digging here, a thorn digging there, and a thorn digging somewhere else. There are thorns everywhere.

Is not that exactly what thorn-bush brethren are like? Thorns, sticking out all over them. The kind of man you are afraid to go near in the meeting because he is sure to be complaining about something or somebody and nothing in the assembly is ever right. He is always complaining, of course, that no one shows him any fellowship. The reason for this is that it is dangerous to be near him. You can't love a thorn-bush. You don't take a thorn-bush and squeeze it to your breast. Why, it would prick you all over! Thorn-bush brethren — you are almost afraid to smile at them, afraid to say 'good morning' to them, because you wonder what is going to come out next. If you try to shelter under a thorn-bush, my dear brother, you'll get pricked!

Remember the bramble-bushes of the assembly are like Abimelech of our chapter: always seeking supporters, always seeking followers, wanting the men of Shechem to back them up and to plead their cause. The men of Shechem found that Abimelech was a thorn-bush, didn't they? We shall read later that Abimelech slew the men of Shechem. They found they had got under a thorn-bush. If you meet this kind of brother, avoid him; if not, you'll get pricked. You say, Are you actually teaching there are members of the assembly we must shun? Have you considered Romans 16:17: "Mark them which cause divisions and offences contrary to the doctrine which ye have learned; and avoid them." So if you have a thorn-bush brother in the meeting who is always complaining, always finding fault, always suggesting that if he had the reins things would be so much better, the Spirit of God says "lean away from him."

What does the Word say? "And the bramble said unto the trees, If in truth ye anoint me king over you, then come and put your trust in my shadow: and if not, let fire come out of the bramble and devour the cedars of Lebanon." If you don't make me king, I will show you how much I love you. If you don't make me king, you'll learn that I don't love you. I love myself, love the place of pre-eminence, and if you don't come under my shadow, then I will burn you up. Is that the kind of man you want for a shepherd in the assembly? A man who says, Either do what I tell you, or else it will be worse for you. A man who is so determined to have his way, to be king, to be a Diotrephes in the assembly, that he doesn't mind how the assembly suffers or how the individuals in the assembly are hurt.

Wasn't Diotrephes like that? He had managed to get a place of dominance over the overseeing brethren. And it seems to me that one day some of the Lord's commended servants came along to that assembly and they had a letter of commendation signed, possibly by the apostle John. Said Diotrephes, We don't want them in here. And he wouldn't have them in the assembly. Why? Because, says the Word of God, "he loved the pre-eminence." He knew that if those men came in they would help the saints, but he would lose his place of pre-eminence. So he said, Mr. Olive, I don't want you here; Mr. Fig, I don't want you here; Mr. Vine, I don't want you here. He had no time for spiritual men. No wonder John said, "When I come"! Prating against John and his associates with malicious words was this man, and John would come with apostolic authority and deal with him.

In these Old Testament passages in the days of the Judges, there was no John to deal with Abimelech. But there was God. My dear brethren and sisters, always remember, when you have in an assembly men who are of the character of Abimelech — so difficult to handle, difficult to get on with, causing trouble wherever they go — when they force themselves into leadership as Abimelech did, please don't despair. Even if you feel you can't do anything about it, just tell the Lord. After all, remember that the assembly is God's assembly.

Sometimes there are situations where the dear brethren feel that they can't do anything more. Well, you just hand it over to God. A solemn scene indeed, when God steps into an assembly and begins to act.

Let us notice now how God stepped into this situation. Verse 22 of chapter 9: "When Abimelech had reigned three years over Israel, then God ..." That's it! Seventy sons of Gideon lay dead. A despot had been crowned among the people. A carnal man surrounded by carnal men, and the whole of them gone over to idolatry. You say the thing is hopeless. It is, until you read "Then God." What did God do? God sent an evil spirit between Abimelech and the men of Shechem. It was through the men of Shechem that Abimelech had obtained the money to pay the vain fellows that put the seventy sons of Gideon to death. Abimelech and the men of Shechem had worked together. This man had pushed himself into the 'oversight' with the support of carnal men. But then God sent an evil spirit between Abimelech and his supporters. That's all. My dear brethren, if you have men in your assembly that cause trouble, just tell the Lord. And wait! The time will come when they will fall out with each other. That is all that happened here. The men of Shechem turned against the man whose cause they had promoted. God put an evil spirit between them.

God, today, can handle His own assembly. He can order His own house. And when there are those who would disturb the peace, bring in strife and trouble and drive out spiritual men, then God can come in and separate the leaders of the trouble from their supporters. I have seen that happen. Doubtless older brethren have seen that happen too. People who act against God always fall out with each other. That's what they did here. When an evil spirit came in between Abimelech and the men of Shechem, they were no longer loyal to him. He had asked for their help to get him into the place of king, but after they had helped he had no more time for them. He had arrived at his objective. He had used them, and they didn't matter anymore. So the evil spirit comes in between him as leader and them as followers, and they dealt treacherously with Abimelech.

Is there a bramble-bush brother who thinks he has the support of some carnal people in the assembly? Remember please that people who will join with you against the overseeing brethren will, in a few days, turn against you. It is their characteristic feature. They are against the oversight and you are against the oversight, so they will support you. But when you become a leader, they will still be against the government and so against you. The Spirit of God shows that they began to deal treacherously with Abimelech. Who? The very people who had dealt treacherously with Gideon's sons. Treacherous people can never be trusted. And the carnal element in an assembly will put into a place of prominence a carnal man, but when he doesn't do what they want, they'll turn against him as well. So thorn-bush men are always in a precarious position. For when they do get a place of prominence among God's people, they get it with the popular support of carnality, and that can never be relied upon.

Now let us proceed to verse 25. "The men of Shechem set liers in wait for him in the top of the mountains, and they robbed all that came along that way." First they deal treacherously, then they are spying. So there comes in between Abimelech and the men of Shechem

10

treachery, spying, suspicion, betraying one another,
robbing one another. And you'll notice please at the end
of verse 25: "And it was told Abimelech." So there was
someone there who was playing two ways. Someone in
touch with the men of Shechem, and running and
telling Abimelech. When it is carnal men you are
dealing with there is nothing they will stop at. Carnal
men and women in the assembly will be treacherous,
will lie in wait to catch their brethren and sisters, and
may even go so far as to rob — rob them of their
characters. How many times have we met people who,
to use another term, "run with the hare and hunt with
the hounds"?

Notice a further development in verse 26. "And Gaal
the son of Ebed came with his brethren, and went over
to Shechem: and the men of Shechem put their
confidence in him." What's this? Oh! Abimelech, he
schemed in order to get the leadership with the support
of carnal men. Now, here comes another carnal man.
And he contacts the men of Shechem and says, "You
know, Abimelech isn't doing all you thought he would
do. He isn't the kind of king you expected him to be. But
follow me." So now there is a rival leader, a rebellion
against Abimelech, or if you like, against Diotrephes.
There is rebellion by a carnal man against the carnal
man who slew the spiritual men. Young believer, let me
tell you that rebellion is never right in an assembly. If
you have spiritual overseers, you'll have no need to
rebel. If you have carnal overseers, you must not rebel.
You say, But if we have got a man like Abimelech who
has pushed himself to the front and he's controlling the
assembly and everything is going wrong, you mean to
say young men are not to rise up and say "Abimelech,

enough"? No, No. This man who rose up against Abimelech failed. His rebellion was an utter failure, and he proved to be only a boaster, nothing but talk. So rebellion in the assembly is a sign of carnality, and you never rebel. Then how will this man be removed? Not by the rebellion of Gaal, but by the poetic justice of God.

Go a little further in the Old Testament to the record of Saul. He's a king, and has been anointed. He's a king that once moved with God though he was a man of the flesh. The time comes when he disobeys God and the Spirit of God leaves him. He is absolutely rejected by God and by Samuel, and turns to the witch of Endor in the end. In contradistinction to him, Samuel has already put the anointing oil upon the head of David. And on two occasions David could have stretched out his hand and taken the life of Saul. On both occasions David reminds himself that it is forbidden to lift up one's hand against the Lord's anointed. But you say, David is the Lord's anointed; Saul has departed from God and is a rejected king. Listen! as long as Saul lived, he'd had the anointing oil upon his head, and though he was rejected and had turned to witchcraft, David would not lift up his hand against the Lord's anointed. Turn over to the next chapter and there you see an Amalekite who dared to slay Saul, and David says, "How wast thou not afraid to stretch forth thine hand to destroy the Lord's anointed?" And on David's instructions he was put to death.

So, if you have a supposed overseer in your company who is the New Testament answer to Abimelech, don't dare to lift up your hand against the Lord's anointed. He has taken a position, and God will hold him responsible for the position he has taken. Never lift up a rebel hand to remove him. Just tell the Lord about it, and you may be surprised how quickly that man's seat will be vacant in the assembly. God can remove him. Solemn, isn't it? You never rebel. You tell the Lord.

So this man Gaal, he raises up himself. Notice please how carnality comes out now. Note the kind of man who will lead the rebellion. It says "he went into the house of their god," — first of all idolatry — and "did eat and drink, and curse Abimelech." So you have an association here now rising up among God's people determined to remove a man of Diotrephes character, but they were blasphemous, drunken and idolatrous. We should never want to be in their company, but let us remember that while carnal saints will not go to these lengths they do have carnal features.

From verse 50 onwards Abimelech is fighting his last battle. He has already slain the people, beaten down the city and sowed it with salt (verse 45). The men of Shechem then entered into the house of their god, Berith, and Abimelech led his followers in an attack. They cut down boughs and used them to burn the tower of Shechem and its occupants — about one thousand men and women died. Oh, the tragic results of carnal leadership! (Did not Jotham say, "Let fire come out of the bramble"?) In verse 50, he proceeds to Thebez and starts to do the same thing: burn down the tower and destroy the people. The inhabitants get inside that tower in order that they might be safe. Verse 52 says, "And Abimelech came unto the tower and fought against it, and went hard unto the door of the tower to burn it with fire. And a certain woman cast a piece of a millstone upon Abimelech's head, and all to brake his skull. Then he called hastily unto the young man his armour-bearer and said unto him, Draw thy sword and slay me, that men say not of me, A woman slew him." This is the poetic justice of God. Abimelech had through his scheming killed the seventy sons of Gideon upon one stone. So we have one stone, and we have the word 'slew'. It's a woman that slays Abimelech with one stone. There was a measure of dignity about the execution of Gideon's sons, but there's only shame about the death of Abimelech. God says, "For whatsoever a man soweth, that shall he also reap." Gideon's sons had doubtless been beheaded ceremonially on one stone. So Abimelech's head is crushed with one stone. That's what happens when God steps in to remove a carnal man who has destroyed God's people. Notice please, he is taken away in shame. What did he say? "Let it not be said that a woman slew him." There is something dignified about a public execution when the executioner is a man, but there is something shameful about death when the one who did it is a woman. So he dies in shame, this man who wanted to be like a thorn-bush waving over the trees of the forest, he dies under the disciplining hand of God, in shame. Let us consider the matter well.

Jephthah — The Legal Judge

Jephthah was a Gileadite, a mighty man of valour. An ideal man to take a sword and be a deliverer of Israel. In fact he is seen to be a mighty man of valour in chapter 11, both at the beginning and in the middle of the chapter, and also in chapter 12. The only difference being that at the start of chapter 11, he's the mighty man of valour proved by past victories, in the middle of the chapter he's a mighty man of valour when he destroys Israel's enemies, but in chapter 12 he is a mighty man of valour when he slays forty-two thousand of his brethren.

It is great to be a mighty man of valour among the people of God, made strong by the Lord Himself, able to do exploits for God. When God's people need a deliverer it is great to be a man that can stand among them and lift the delivering sword, in the power of the Spirit of God. But what a tragedy when a mighty man of valour slays more of his own brethren than he ever slew of the ungodly. A great thing to turn the sword against the enemies of the Lord; an awful thing to use that developed skill to destroy the people of God. That's the tragedy of Jephthah. Forty-two thousand of God's people lay dead at the fords of Jordan. A Christian destroying Christians, a godly man slaying the godly. Instead of fighting the adversary, fighting the people of God. Many a strong man among the saints of God, strong in personality, strong in conviction, strong in warfare against the ungodly, strong in the spreading of the gospel, has ended his days slaying the people of God.

This man had a bad beginning: he was the son of a

harlot. Worse in his beginning than Abimelech, for you remember Gideon had many wives, "seventy children of his body begotten." He had also a concubine in Shechem; and concubinage is, in a way, used of God in the Old Testament scriptures, for Jacob's two wives are associated with two handmaids, and through those four women the house of Israel was built. Such concubinage existed in Old Testament days not by divine authority, but by divine permission. Jephthah, however, was the son of a harlot. In other words, while Abimelech was a carnal man, Jephthah was a doubly carnal man — his beginning was base. The Old Testament scriptures are extremely clear about a child of that character: an illegitimate child shall not come into the congregation unto the tenth generation.

It is good to notice another distinction between the two men. Abimelech — the only god he knows is Baal-berith, the god of the land, opposed to the God of Israel. He never once, in the divine record, mentions the name of the Lord. But Jephthah who had such a bad beginning uses the title 'Lord' on a number of occasions, and shows a very full appreciation of who God is. For instance: chapter 11 verse 9, "and the Lord deliver"; verse 11, "and Jephthah uttered all his words before the Lord"; verse 21, "the Lord God of Israel"; verse 23, "the Lord God of Israel"; verse 24, "the Lord our God"; verse 27, "the Lord the Judge"; verse 29, "the Spirit of the Lord came upon him"; verse 30, "he vowed to the Lord"; verse 31, "shall surely be the Lord's"; then in verse 35, "I have opened my mouth unto the Lord." So Jephthah knew the Lord. To Jephthah, God is Jehovah. He is Jehovah of Israel, and you'll notice that He is Jehovah the Judge, and so on. So he has a great appreciation of God as Jehovah, the One who made a covenant with Israel based on sacrifice.

The difference therefore between Abimelech and Jephthah is that Jephthah knows God and Abimelech does not. Abimelech is a picture of an unsaved man and he has only the features of the natural man. Jephthah, in spite of his bad background, knows the Lord and in a sense he loves the Lord, he wants to give something to the Lord. Notice he is a believer on whom the Spirit of the Lord comes; he is similar to Gideon, he knows what it is to move in the power of the Spirit of God.

The unkind attitude of his brethren when he was young had left him with a permanent grudge. This was not removed when he got to know the Lord as his redeemer. There are certain things that are characteristic features, almost built into our make-up. Even after we trust Christ as Saviour we find that these particular features are still with us. If folks have a strange reaction to life before they are saved they often have it after they are saved. Some folks have had a very bad temper before they were saved and they have great difficulty in suppressing it afterwards. By the grace of God they can keep it under, but their basic disposition does not alter. So when I consider Jephthah, he is a strange mixture: naturally — with a grudge; spiritually — a man who knows the Lord, wants to serve Him, wants to fight for Him. All through his life these two facets of his character fight each other. Yet there are facets of divine grace in the man which you must admire. And the Spirit of God admires them, for in Hebrews chapter 11 you find him in the portrait gallery of the men of faith.

One is glad to find a man like this in the Bible because you and I are something like that too. There are so many features I had before I was saved, and while divine grace helps me to suppress them, so often they come through. There's always a battle going on in my life as to whether it is those awful features of the old thing, or those lovely features of Christ, that manifest themselves. Will you not agree with me, dear child of God, that that has been your history? You want to be more like Christ, want to show more and more of His love and beauty and grace day by day. You mourn in the presence of God time and time again that certain facets of your character that are undesirable, will come through.

How did he develop this unfortunate attitude? He could't help being born of a harlot. It had nothing to do with him. With tender hearts we might say, he is an object to be pitied, an object to be cared for, an object to be taken in and loved. Those are lovely sentiments, but that is not what happened to this young man. Gilead's wife bare him sons; but Gilead also had a son born of a harlot and apparently he brought that son home into his own house and brought him up as one of the family. But when Gilead's sons grew up, that is, his sons born of his rightful wife, "they drave out Jephthah" saying "Thou shalt not inherit in our father's house; for thou art the son of a strange woman." Jephthah was the victim of animosity, a most unhappy child, in possibly an unhappy home. It was the result of his fathers immorality.

Do you think it was right that Jephthah's brothers cast him out like that? All our sentiments would be against that. Our sentiments would be to love him, be kind to him, care for him. But Jephthah's brothers didn't think that way at all. What did they do? They thrust him out. Do you suppose they could quote

Scripture for what they did? Could they not take into their hands the Mosaic law and say "that an illegitimate child should not be brought into the assembly to the tenth generation"? A scriptural principle? at least, if not a scripture, to support the unkind way in which they ejected Jephthah from their home. They could say, "God said you must not bring him into the assembly for ten generations. Therefore we'll not have him in our home." They could also find a worthy example for it. In the book of Genesis Abraham and his association with Hagar produced Ishmael. First of all, you'll remember that Abraham, under Sarah's instructions, sent away Hagar when she was expecting the child. She came home and remained for a number of years, but the final words were authenticated from heaven, "Cast out the bondwoman and her son, for her son shall not inherit with Isaac." So, they had both: a scripture and a scriptural principle for what they did. Ah! but behind all this they had something else, and that was the real reason for their behaviour. It was not obedience to God's word that motivated them. It was love of self, love of money — greed! Notice what they said, "Thou shalt not inherit in our father's house, for thou art the son of a strange woman." What was the real reason why they cast him out? If Gilead wasn't already dead, he would eventually die and there would be something to inherit. They said, If we let Jephthah remain here he'll take part of the inheritance and we are going to see to it that he doesn't.

Had they thought a little bit deeper, they could have said, Yes, the Lord does say you must not bring in an illegitimate child till the tenth generation, but Pharez was an illegitimate child to whom grace was shown.

Rahab was a harlot, but she was the subject of grace. Ruth, she was a Moabitess and she must not come in until the tenth generation, but she's brought into the kingly line. So we learn from the Old Testament scriptures that grace has, on occasions, triumphed over law.

Jephthah's brothers could have put a pious smile upon their faces and quoted the Scripture in order to justify their dastardly deed when they put Jephthah out of the family home. The reason they did it however was not to be obedient to the Scriptures, nor to please the Lord: it was covetousness. That's what legality is. Legality is when we put on a holy face, a pious smile, maybe we speak in our most sanctimonious tones, and we make something we want to do appear spiritual; but deep down in our hearts our motive is not to please the Lord, but to benefit ourselves. Legality quotes the Scripture. Legality boasts divine principle. But it comes from a hardened heart that is not concerned about pleasing the Lord, but benefiting oneself and getting one's own way. That's what Jephthah's brethren did, and it has been done thousands of times since! With a Scripture on our lips, maybe a principle from Scripture and it sounds so right, but in the man's heart who is arguing the case there's hardness, maybe there is hatred, maybe he is wanting to do his brother or sister an injury; and the God who reads the heart sees covetousness, love of self, love of our own way.

Jephthah becomes a mighty man of valour. Verse 3 says he is a leader of vain fellows; they went out together. And the passage seems to suggest that Jephthah became a kind of brigand leader. This would appear to be the reaction to the way he had been treated by normal society. Still a mighty man of valour, but because he has been turned out from home and hearth, he becomes a brigand on the hills. A leader of empty worthless men, but a mighty man of valour. The elders of Israel heard of him and, in an emergency when the children of Ammon made war against Israel, they realised they really needed a mighty man of valour to step in and deliver them. Knowing of Jephthah's skill as a brigand on the hills they made their way into the land of Tob to obtain his help.

Now read verse 7: "And Jephthah said unto the elders of Gilead, Did not ye hate me, and expel me out of my father's house? and why are ye come unto me now when ye are in distress?" Jephthah has not forgotten or forgiven. He's going back to that beginning, to the way they treated him and despised him and cast him out of the house. I suppose many years have passed since then. He is a trained brigand on the hills, he knows the way to fight battles, he knows he can deliver Israel. His attitude is, "You wouldn't have me years ago, but you want me now. You put me out of the house because you wanted the money, now when you are in difficulties you beg me to come back and fight for you. Do you think I'm going to help you? You didn't want me then and I won't help you now." Tit for tat. The way they treated him — no time for you, Jephthah, you're not having any of our money — but now they are in need and he rejects their overtures.

I wonder if there are any of us like that. We carry a grudge, sometimes for years. A Sunday School superintendent was required in the assembly and you thought you could do that, but they passed you by. In a few years' time they'll again need a superintendent. And will you say, "You passed me by last time, you did not want me, I won't help you now. Have you forgotten, you turned me down last time? Do you think I am going to do anything to help you?" Have you ever met any people like that? Maybe you are a teacher, and there was a need in the assembly for someone to speak on a certain subject because the saints needed help on that. My brother, you just thought you could do that well, didn't you? But the brethren thought of somebody else and overlooked you. Now the Lord has taken the other dear man to heaven, and again they want someone to speak on a special subject, and they come to you and say, "Brother, would you like to take up such and such a subject? The saints need your help," and you say, "Remember when you turned me down long ago? You didn't what my help then. Do you think you can just pick me up and lay me down when you like? Find somebody else." That's the type of man Jephthah was. Ah! he says, you turned me out when I was a young fellow, you wanted my money: well, you can just get on without me now, for I have had enough. Jephthah's a man in a huff because they turned him out. Jephthah's not dead yet! There are saints that act in this way because in the past they have not been given the place of importance they supposed they ought to have had; and when the saints really need them they say, "Just remember the way you treated me. I'm having nothing to do with it."

But was he right? had he a scriptural principle for acting this way? Let us read the previous chapter and see that Jephthah is almost repeating the words of God. After God's people had forsaken the Lord and served Balaam they cried unto the Lord and they said, "We have sinned," and the Lord said to them in verses 13 and 14, "Yet ye have forsaken me and served other gods: wherefore I will deliver you no more. Go and cry unto the gods which ye have chosen; let them deliver you in the time of your tribulation." That's what God said. Here are these people crying for deliverance and God says, "Did I not deliver you? ... You cried unto me and I delivered you out of their hand. Yet ye have forsaken me and served other gods. Wherefore I will save you no more. Go and cry unto the gods which ye have chosen, let them deliver you in the time of your distress" (vv. 11-14). That's what God did. Why did He do that? Here is the point. God had a reason for doing that: He wanted them to confess again "We have sinned." He wanted their repentance to be real. They did say it again, and they proved the reality of their words. I read, "And they put away the strange gods from among them, and served the Lord: and His soul was grieved for the misery of Israel." Why had God allowed trouble to come upon them? It was His discipline. Why does God discipline His people? Because He loves them; His motives are the very best: He loves them. When He disciplines His people what does it say? "His soul was grieved for the misery of Israel." That was God's attitude to Israel. He lifts a parental hand and smites His erring child, and when His erring child cries out in pain His soul is distressed, grieved for the misery of Israel. It is almost as though the God of heaven weeps, is moved to compassion as He hears the deep, deep cries of His people: because He loves them. Because He loves them He disciplines them for their good, but when He sees them suffering beneath His disciplining hand, it grieves His loving heart.

God doesn't want to discipline His people, but He does it. As a faithful Father He disciplines every son whom He receiveth, but He doesn't find any enjoyment in doing it — His soul is grieved for the misery of His people. That's why God said to them, Now, you've been serving these gods all those years, and now you come to me; go back to them! But God was saying that, not out of selfishness, not out of unkindness. There is no attitude of "you haven't wanted me, so just get on the best you can." There is no spirit like that about God. He was acting because He loved them.

So, in our chapter Jephthah does precisely the same. He says, You've been getting on well without me since the day you thrust me out. Just get on without me now when you are in trouble. He was doing exactly what God did. But wait a minute: the motive was different, wasn't it? On the surface there is a similarity between Jephthah's attitude and God's. But God was doing it because He loved His people; Jephthah was acting that way because he loved himself. That was the difference. And so again legality appears on the surface to be godly. It talks sanctimoniously and appears to be imitating God's attitude. But God's attitude was love to His people. Jephthah's was love of Jephthah. He wanted, like Diotrephes, the pre-eminence, the first place; and he says, You can all be slain on the battlefield if you like, and I'll not help you, unless you make me king. He didn't love God's people, he loved himself; and he was only willing to help if they made him "head".

I wonder, do we really love God's people, or do we love the pre-eminence? For sometimes, like Jephthah, we may even argue like God; but God's motives are pure and full of love and meant for the good of His people.

Sometimes our motives are impure, can be full of animosity, not meant for the good of God's people but for the exaltation of self. That's what I mean by legality. In years of experience among God's people, how often have I heard a man with a religious argument upon his lips — scriptural reasoning, scriptural phraseology. Knowing the type of man he is, I say to myself, Brother, what you are saying with your lips is not what you are thinking in your heart. There's an ulterior motive behind an apparently scriptural argument — and that's legality.

A man who talks that way is a strange man, you'll agree. But a man who eventually is persuaded — yes, he has to be persuaded! — to become head of God's people. Oh! he wants to be, mark you. He says, I'm only prepared to do it if you make me chief. And they have to persuade him to become chief at the end. The New Testament tells me that overseers should never have to be persuaded to be overseers, they should never have to be pressed into the work. "Taking the oversight thereof, not by constraint, but willingly, not for filthy lucre, but of a ready mind" (1 Peter 5:2). The Holy Spirit makes them overseers, and because they love the saints and they see the saints are in danger they say, We'll go out and fight for them. They don't have to be bribed, they don't have to be constrained, oh no! Jephthah had to be, and he was only willing if he could be chief. A real shepherd of God's people never needs to be asked, never needs to be told. If God's people are in danger he'll be there to defend them, and when it is done he will fade out of the picture. He won't want any glory for it at all. He'll do it because he loves the saints. But a legal man loves to be persuaded, loves to be pushed, makes demands for elevation — that's legality! So, eventually they made him king.

The middle of chapter 11 introduces us to another strong facet of this man's character: he's talking to the Lord's enemies. He talks to them from the end of verse 12 down to the end of verse 28. Observe please, that this man who has to be constrained, persuaded, given headship in order to become a deliverer of God's people, proves to be most difficult when dealing with the people of God. He spends a long time quietly reasoning with the enemies of God's people. That's strange, isn't it? Quietly reasoning with the enemies of God's people. They say in politics it's better to talk than to fight, and Jephthah apparently believed that. So, in all these verses he talks to the enemies of the Lord, trying to convince them that they were wrong and that his cause was right. And only when his lengthy discourse has failed did the children of Ammon and he join battle.

I find that there are some dear men who are great men at giving out tracts, great men at carrying text banners, great men at personal conversation, and they are prepared to talk to unsaved men and women most graciously for a long time and the Lord blesses their efforts. But in the assembly when something doesn't suit them they almost explode with bad temper. Have you ever met any men like that? Lots of patience when it is the unsaved, willing to plead and to pray when it is those outside, but very difficult to get on with in the assembly. My dear fellow saint, your first duty is to the saints of God, your first duty is to love the brethren. You should be the easiest possible man or woman to get on with among the saints of God; then carry that kindness out to the world. I suppose sometimes earthly families are like

11

that — inside the family home they argue and dispute, outside they are all love. There are some folks among the saints of God like that. Jephthah was a man who would reason and plead to prevent warfare, trying to care for those outside, but showing practically no love to those inside. That's the spirit of legality.

We must consider the major problem in the life of Jephthah, that is, what he did with his daughter. Notice please that the man who is legal is a rash man. The book of Leviticus talks about men speaking rashly with their lips: "If a soul swear rashly with his lips to do evil or to do good, whatsoever it be that a man shall pronounce rashly with an oath ..." (Leviticus 5:4). Speaking rashly, he vowed a vow unto the Lord, namely, "If thou shalt without fail deliver the children of Ammon into my hands, then it shall be that whosoever [not whatsoever] cometh forth of the doors of my house to meet me ..." Whosoever? what's this? Here's a man who says, Whatever living person comes out of my house when I come back, I'll offer him or her in sacrifice. Doubtless he thought that he would see coming out of his house one of his lower servants, some bondservant, maybe of another nation, that had been taken into his family to be a slave. If it were a slave coming out of his house, it was going to cost him practically nothing to sacrifice that slave to the Lord. But rash words will often come home to sit on our own doorstep. And you know the story: that out of his house came his only daughter. Legal men go in for rash words. Legal men are willing to sacrifice others; they don't mind if others suffer. Have you ever heard a legal man when somebody else's family is not behaving as it should? He says, Do this, or this, or this; and there is not a bit of love or mercy about the man. But one day the same thing comes home to sit on his own doorstep and his own family do the same thing. Does the principle of sowing and reaping apply?

My brethren, we should always be careful what we say, for many a man that ministers often has to eat his own ministry. You can't minister on a subject to the saints of God without practically, in your own life, being put to the test on that very ministry. Here is a man who stood and said publicly before the Lord that he would give the first living thing that came out of his house. God brought it right home to his own doorstep. The price of legality can be very bitter, can be very costly: and it was going to cost Jephthah his only daughter. The rashness of a legal man!

You ask me what I think he did? From the type of man I see Jephthah to be in Judges chapters 11 and 12, I believe he sacrificed his daughter. You see, he is a legal man, a self-important man; and a legal man mustn't lose face. He stood and said, Lord, I'll give you the first thing that comes out of my house. The people will say, We heard him say it, now we'll watch and see if he does it. His legality is tearing at his broken heart, yet he mustn't lose face. He must not appear before the people of God as a man who changed his mind, and though it was breaking his heart a legal man must carry it through. Many a legal man has destroyed his own wife and family and by his hardness of heart has lost his family for God, rather than admit that he was wrong and that in the past he had been too hard. Rather than lose face Jephthah sacrificed his daughter. (You may think that he merely committed her to perpetual virginity — either way the teaching is just the same.)

You ask, Could he have done anything else? I think he

could. What does Leviticus 5:4 make provision for? It
talks about a sacrifice for a vow. It's a trespass offering
and it has to do with a vow. Do you not need the trespass
offering if you fail to keep the vow? But as a legal man he
could not search out a way in which, through grace and
sacrifice, he could save his daughter's life, because he
would lose face. And he'd rather sacrifice his daughter
than lose face. That's a legal man, a hard-hearted
character: he won't bend. He was reared in a hard-
hearted home. He steeled his heart to the needs of God's
people and said, I won't go and fight for you unless you
make me chief. Now he steels his heart and sacrifices his
daughter. He's a legal man.

Chapter 12 tells me that the men of Ephraim came
and chided with him sharply. Remember Gideon had
the same experience? The Ephraimites complained to
him in precisely the same way. Gideon dealt wisely with
the situation. He proved that "a soft answer turneth
away wrath." But a legal man doesn't do that; he will
reason with the enemy (chapter 11:12-28), but has no
patience with those of his own nation. He sticks up for
his rights, and seeing that he has been the great general
who won the war he is not going to give someone else the
credit. Oh no! he is going to have his rights, and before
anybody could think Jephthah has taken his sword and
the battle has started and he's slaying God's people.
Ever seen legal men doing that? There is not a bit of love
about them, just slaying God's people. What does a legal
man finally do? He takes his men to the fords of Jordan
and says, This is the way you'll do it: tell them to say
"shibboleth". And the Ephraimites couldn't say 'sh'
they could only say 'si'. "He could not frame to
pronounce it right" (v. 6). Everyone that said "sibboleth"

they slew. What did they do? They slew a man because he couldn't pronounce one letter right — that's legality! And legality among the saints thousands of times since has slain fellow brethren and sisters because they couldn't say one word right. That is legality. The man who stands for rights, the man who tries to argue that what he does is scripturally right, and that covers the evil of his own heart. Because he doesn't really love God's people in the way that he should, but only loves himself: instead of lifting them up he leaves forty-two thousand dead bodies at the fords of Jordan.

Jephthah judges Israel six years. Six years of triumph and tragedy, six years marred by legality. The Lord deliver us from legality!

Samson — The Strong, Weak Judge

One would almost wonder how Samson ever came to be reckoned among the men of faith when you think of the mistakes he made, the wrong things he did, the strange way he finished; but in Hebrews 11:32 we read "Time would fail to tell of Gideon, Barak, Samson or Jephthah ... who through faith ..." In the close of Judges 15 you do read this, "And he judged Israel in the days of the Philistines twenty years." So, while the Word of God says a lot about his mistakes, it does seem that there was a period in the middle of his life when he judged Israel. He must have done it by faith, for the New Testament commends him for it. Now Judges chapter 13 gives you the events just prior to his history. "And the children of Israel did evil again in the sight of the Lord; and the Lord delivered them into the hands of the Philistines forty years. And there was a certain man of Zorah, of the family of the Danites, whose name was Manoah; and his wife was barren, and bare not. And the angel of the Lord appeared unto the woman, and said unto her, Behold now, thou art barren, and bearest not: but thou shalt conceive, and bear a son. Now therefore beware, I pray thee, and drink not wine nor strong drink, and eat not any unclean thing: for, lo, thou shalt conceive, and bear a son; and no razor shall come on his head: for the child shall be a Nazarite unto God from the womb: and he shall begin to deliver Israel out of the hand of the Philistines. Then the woman came and told her husband, saying, A man of God came unto me, and his countenance was like the countenance of an angel of

God, very terrible: but I asked him not whence he was, neither told he me his name: but he said unto me, Behold, thou shalt conceive, and bear a son; and now drink no wine nor strong drink, neither eat any unclean thing: for the child shall be a Nazarite to God from the womb to the day of his death.''

Notice please, that the enemy in the days of Samson was the Philistine and they became the dominant enemy not only for the rest of the Book of Judges, but for the earliest chapters of the Book of Samuel. Let us remind ourselves what the Philistines represent. Their origin may be rather obscure: some think they came from an island in the Mediterranean. Anyway, in the course of their journey they made their way to Egypt and from Egypt they seem to have wandered into the land of Palestine which is first of all called Philistia — the land of the Philistines. From Egypt to Canaan they had gone, but they only wandered there, for the Philistines are the wanderers. When they left Egypt it was not because they had been building brick-kilns and feeling the lash. It wasn't that God sent Moses to them to bring them out. They had not had the experience of being sheltered by passover blood, neither had they miraculously passed through the Red Sea. They had not wandered for forty years in the wilderness, nor had they miraculously crossed Jordan. But, they were in the land! and they were in the land of which God says that His eye rests upon it from the beginning of the year to the end, that He has put His name upon it and put His throne in the centre of it. They had arrived in that land!

The children of Israel, they also in the course of their journeyings arrived in Egypt and eventually came to that same land where God had placed His Name, where

God was King. But their journey through had been different, they had known the brick-kilns and the lash, and redemption by blood; they crossed the Red Sea miraculously and were pilgrims and strangers for a long time in the wilderness. They crossed Jordan on dry land and had arrived, shall we say, home. The history of each of these is entirely different, and that will explain to us the meaning of the word Philistines when we apply it to the present day. Both Philistines and Israelites commenced in Egypt, both arrived in the place where God had placed His Name, but the way they journeyed was different!

You and I profess rightly to have got to where God has placed His Name. If you like, we are in God's land, we're enjoying our inheritance. Ah! but leave this hall and wander abroad, and you'll find there are a lot of other folk and they started in the same Egypt as we did, now they are in a building where it says, "The Church of this or The Church of that," or they've taken a Bible name and tagged it on. What does the Church mean? A called-out company. So, they've got a name that's a Bible name. If you went to them and asked them what their church was, they'd say it was the church that was established by our Lord long, long ago. They started in Egypt and they are in a place today that has the name of God on it and professes the name of Christ. We call it Christendom. It's got the name of Christ on it and it's got "dom" on the end of it — the domain of Christ. You say, That's where we are. That's right, and that's where they are. We both start in the same place and we both finish, professedly, in the same place. Oh! but the journey we took is different from theirs; isn't it? We knew the conviction of sin, in other words, we felt the burden of our bondage. They, they never thought Egypt was a bad place, they enjoyed its melons, its leeks, its garlic, its onions. They didn't want to get out of Egypt. We wanted to get out of Egypt, we felt the burden of sin, the bondage, the lash; and we may even have wept because of our sins. But Philistines never realised they were sinners. We felt the need of being sheltered by blood; but if I asked a Philistine if his sins were washed away, he would say, Disgusting language that, fancy thinking of getting your sins "washed in the blood of the Lamb" — barbarous. They put no value on the blood, but we do. We realised that when Christ died, He died for me — blessed truth. Philistines have never realised yet that they are sinners and deserved to die, and as for the cross of Christ having any personal application, they never heard of such a thing and they certainly don't believe it. We see this world as a wilderness and go through it as pilgrims and strangers; but they say, This world is where we belong: we are happy here. We've come to the Jordan and not only learned Red Sea truth: that Christ died for me, but Jordan truth: I died with Christ. But they are very much alive and everything that is in the world pleases them, it's second nature to them. We died to it, at least, we professed to in our baptism, didn't we? But they never died to it. Self —they like to indulge it. Sin — they like to practise it. The world — they want to enjoy it. Yes, but we are both in the same place. I don't mean in assembly fellowship, don't misunderstand me. I mean they've got into the land with the name of Christ on it and the name of God on it — Christendom. The church, professedly, in contradistinction to that which is the true church of God; members of the true church of God are all born again.

The enemy in this chapter is the Philistine holding down God's people. Christendom holding down true born-again Christians is a picture of many of our dear brethren and sisters today that find themselves in various denominations that are not in accord with the Scriptures. In many of them the men who occupy the pulpit have never been born again — they are Philistines. While in the pews often sit born-again children of God, robbed of their freedom, robbed of the exercise of their priesthood, robbed of the exercise of whatever gifts God may have given them, and robbed of what is theirs in the liberty of Christ: because Philistines have them under their domination.

Samson was going to find that Philistines were strange folk. One of the first Philistines he saw, he thought she was lovely. So he married her and found what kind of person his father-in-law was. One of our dear Irish brethren said, "If you marry an unconverted person, you'll have the Devil for your father-in-law." Samson found that the attractiveness of some Philistine girl only led him to a circle of people who did most gruesome things. Philistines are like that: lovely people, educated people, refined people, religious people — they present almost the greatest danger to God's people in the day in which we live. They are so attractive and refined, but get on the wrong side of them and it's a different story.

All through the Word of God you'll find that the religious folk are the greatest opponents of the things of God — Philistines. You remember those men in the Book of Nehemiah: Sanballat, Tobiah, and Geshom the Arabian, ah! all representing the same thing as the Philistines, the biggest opponents of the work of God in that day.

Young man, never be enticed by a pretty Philistine face. Young woman, never be enticed by a handsome Philistine man. In the end Philistines put the eyes out of the saints of God. They will rob you of spiritual eyesight, put you in prison, rob you of freedom. That's what this lesson tells us, that is what happened to Samson.

Given that as a background, it was necessary that God should raise up a man to deliver His people from the Philistines. Tragic thing if he fail. We read together, "By him the Lord began." But he was so occupied with getting mixed up with the Philistines that he forgot to fight them. So he began, but he never finished. Young man, young woman, let me repeat, it is a good thing to begin well. He began — "The Spirit of God began to move him." He only began, and the life that finished with tragedy began with the brightest hopes.

You might be reading these lines today and the elder brethren from your assembly say, We thank God for that young man, we thank God for that young woman. Maybe in a few years' time they won't be saying that. Maybe they will weep about you, pray about you. The charge against the church of Sardis in Revelation chapter 3 is "thy works are not perfected before God." Sardis started, went on, but didn't finish. Let us be warned about being good beginners, but early failures; that's what Samson was.

Now, God raised up a man to "deliver his people out of the hand of the Philistines." "There was a certain man of Zorah" (that word means "nest of hornets"), "of the family of the Danites" (that is the worst tribe), "whose name was Manoah" (that means rest), "and his wife" (that stands for weakness) "was barren" (no

fruitfulness). That's the background of the raising up of
Samson. I submit you couldn't get anything worse. If
you had wanted to be in despair about God's people in
that day, you'd have looked at that family. There was
evidently no hope of a deliverer for God's people coming
from there. While you might have looked in many
another place, you wouldn't have looked there. The
impossibility of the situation is impressed upon you. So
often the Book of Judges would teach us this story: that it
is when we come to an end of self, to the end of our
resources, and the situation seems to be absolutely
impossible, it is then God starts. He starts with the
impossible! When we've come to the end of our tether.
The hymn says, "When we have exhausted our hoard of
resources," it is then "He giveth, and giveth, and giveth
again." This idea is the prelude to all revival. The way
to revival is to realise that we are nothing, we are empty
and barren, useless. It's when we realise there is no
sufficiency in ourselves that we can say, "Our sufficiency
is of God who has made us sufficient ministers." For all
the sufficiency in divine things must come from God. If
God's people in our day are needing men who will be
real God-given leaders, it will only happen when we
come to the point where we say, "Lord, we have failed,
we have made a mess of things, we haven't taught as we
should, haven't preached as we should, we are helpless
and absolutely dependent on Thee, Lord, to move."
That's when revival comes!

A nest of hornets — an awful place to be. I'm not
sure if it is a bite or a sting from a hornet, but if you were
in a hornet's nest, whatever way you turned, you would
find it uncomfortable. Do you agree with me that a
hornet is a picture of that which is satanic: attacking

here, attacking there — the darts of the evil one. I
suppose many of us fold our arms on occasions, put on a
smug look and say, "The devil is so busy today." So this
was where Manoah lived. "A nest of hornets" — they
were all round him, they were biting or stinging from all
angles, and you would have said the devil's never been
as busy as he was in Manoah's day. Do you recognize,
dear child of God, that the devil is extremely busy in
these latter times? Says Paul in 1 Timothy, "seducing
spirits"; Paul says to Corinth, "servants of Satan
transforming themselves as angels of light". (The devil
never was so busy as he is today.) Then you say, "That
makes it absolutely impossible for us to do anything
great for God. Look at how powerful the devil is." Wait
a minute! My New Testament says, "He that is in you is
greater than he that is in the world." He that is in you —
the Holy Spirit. He that is in them — the spirit of
antichrist. He that is in you is greater, so there is no
excuse for us comforting ourselves in our inactivity, by
saying the devil is stronger today than ever he was.

Have a good look at **Dan**. The Spirit of God always
gives you the idea of twelve tribes. But, you see, there
were twelve sons, and then Joseph had two sons, and
Manasseh and Ephraim were given a tribe each. That
makes thirteen. God always says twelve. In fact, some
people believe (they may or may not be right) that the
second beast in the Book of Revelation is going to come
from the tribe of Dan. Of Dan, Genesis chapter 49 says
however, "Dan shall be a serpent by the way, an adder
[or horn snake] in the path, that biteth the horses heels,
so that his rider shall fall backwards." In other words,
the tribe of Dan is the treacherous tribe. Treacherous to
his brethren, trying to catch them out and bring them

down. Dan was the farthest from Jerusalem you could get and still be within the borders of the land. Dan was the centre of idolatry in early days. So here is a man, and he lives in a nest of hornets and belongs to the tribe of Dan — the tribe of Dan, treacherous, base, the worst of all the tribes. In other words, Manoah pictures for us a man who lives in the midst of satanic opposition, and when he looks inside he is more than conscious that in himself, in his flesh, dwelleth no good thing.

The devil is so busy all around us, and we are such failures and so incompetent and alas, so sinful. There is really nothing we could expect God to do with material like us.

But then Manoah means **rest**. A strange man to rest in a nest of hornets, a strange man to rest when his conscience was constantly probing him with the fact he had Danite connections. Strange to see saints of God at rest when the devil is busy all around, and strange they can rest when their conscience probes them about their unworthiness and their sinfulness. Why, these two things should have stirred the man to action, but he was at rest — lethargic, indifferent, couldn't care less.

Is our expressed concern about satanic activity just something to ease our conscience, because we are not active? Our confessions of our wrong-doing, instead of driving us to our knees for mercy, are merely excuses for not getting right with God and for going on in the same old routine of lethargy and carelessness, instead of wakefulness and watchfulness. Is that not what is wrong with the assemblies? We know these things, we know that in the last days Satan will be energetic, we know when we look inside how much failure and sin there is: but instead of contrition and repentance driving us into the presence of God, we are apathetic, we lie down among the dead, and you couldn't tell the difference between us and the ungodly; we are like Sardis: "a name to live, but dead."

Add to these things that the Spirit of God passes by the man altogether: He goes to a woman. Now, a woman represents weakness. Not mental weakness, not spiritual weakness, but physical weakness. Go to Peter's epistle: he had a wife, a wife's mother, so he had experience in family life. He's talking about husbands and wives dwelling together and being heirs together of the grace of life — not eternal life, just the grace of living. With the grace of living God is pleased to add little ones to the family, and so husband and wife are heirs together of the grace of life. Now, Peter says, remember that in the matter of bearing children and rearing children and in the running of a home, remember, my dear brother, to give honour unto the weaker vessel. Give respect, give care, show kindness. Why? Because your wife is physically weaker. So you'll do all the chores! In the Word of God the woman is weaker in that sense, and bringing that over as a key to the Old Testament scriptures, wherever you have a woman the thought is weakness.

What a list! A nest of hornets, tribe of Dan, absolute indifference, now weakness. You see, the Spirit of God is spelling out the circumstances of the time for us — impossible circumstances. A woman, though weak, should be fruitful; but she is barren. It's getting worse! And has there been anything of the miraculous in her life relative to this? No! she bare not. The Spirit of God has come down right as far as He can go to say, "Impossible!" I repeat, when the saints of God get there,

God can do something. When Abraham looked at his wife and then at his own body and said, "Impossible!" — God promised a son. When Job was robbed of all his possessions and all his sons and daughters and he longed to die because life in the future seemed impossible, God gave twice as many children and twice as many possessions. When Jacob was at the brook Jabbok and his thigh had gone out of joint and he couldn't struggle anymore he said, "Impossible!" God said, "I'll bless you." When you get there — to the point of impossibility, to the place where you are beaten and defeated and you can't do anything — then God steps in. It's a grand thing when God brings us there, isn't it?

It's at such a time that the angel of the Lord appears to Manoah. Notice please, that "the angel of the Lord", verse 3, is called "a man of God" in verse 6; he is called "the angel of the Lord" in verse 9; then he is "a man" in verses 10 and 11; "the angel of the Lord" in verse 15; his name is "wonderful" in verse 18; and in verse 22, his name is "God". Notice what he is like. His countenance was like the countenance of an angel of God, very terrible. This man is a Christophany, a pre-incarnate appearance of the Lord Jesus, called a man, a man of God, the angel of God, with a terrible countenance; and He is wonderful and He is God. You don't need me to tell you that Isaiah chapter 9 says: "His name shall be called Wonderful." Mark chapter 6 — lovely connection — they say, "Is not this the carpenter?" Have you ever seen a carpenter's hands? — corny, cut, rough. Is that what the hands of your Saviour were like? They say, "See what wondrous works were accomplished by His hands." And so His name is wonderful and Mark says the things He does are wonderful. No doubt about that, it is the Lord Jesus here.

Well now, the angel of the Lord comes to the woman and he tells the woman how to prepare for Israel's deliverer from the Philistines. All of us look forward to the future, that is, if the Lord does not come: and we know that we shall need men in the assemblies of God's people. We'll need men that can preach the gospel, men that can minister God's Word. We'll need men who will be real shepherds of God's people. And every young couple should have an exercise before God, not only that God would give them children. That's only a maternal and paternal desire, but it's right of course. It is wrong for young Christians to anticipate marriage relationships before they have been joined in holy matrimony; it is equally wrong for young Christians to decide not to have children. So you will recognize, young Christians, that children in a home is the natural and scriptural thing. But how about praying for boys? because God needs preachers and teachers, and the assemblies need overseers. Ever thought about praying that you might have men-children? Hannah prayed for a man-child. Here God is preparing the nest again for a man-child.

Would there be anything wrong in young couples praying that God would give them men-children? Not only men-children, but men-children that they might be able to rear for God to be the leaders we will need in coming days. Here in this chapter we have instructions to prepare a nest in which there is going to be born and reared a man to deliver God's people. My dear young brother and sister, would you like to be the parents of a man like that? Would you like to rear someone like that for God in your home? Then you must prepare the nest! My dear elder brethren, you have to be both nursing mothers and school-master fathers in the assembly; the local assembly is a family picture. Would you like to see young men growing up in your assembly to be something for God? You'll need to prepare the nest. God does sometimes raise up men in spite of circumstances. More often He will raise up men where God's people have prepared the nest in which to nurse them.

Notice what kind of nurse: no wine, no strong drink, no unclean thing to be eaten. When the child is born: no razor for his head. Three very simple things that must characterize the home or the assembly that will produce men who will be something for God in a future day. No wine — none of the intoxicating joys of earth. No unclean thing — none of the defiling filth of earth. This is to be a characteristic feature of the homes of God's people; that's pretty plain, isn't it? Notice please, they got this ready before the child was born: so the child could never look back in his life to a moment when defiling things filled the home. No, they hadn't been there all of his life. He could never look back to the intoxication of wine; that had never been present in his house. Unclean things never had place in that circle.

My dear brother, you are the head of the house after all. Don't blame your wife if there is any of the defiling filth of the world in your home. My brother, are there any of the intoxicating joys of earth in your home? You say, Surely you wouldn't think any of us would have any of the filth of the world in our home? Well, I judge not. But how about those intoxicating joys of earth? Are you willing, my dear brother, my dear young sister, to put them all out in order that that child that God might give you will be reared in an atmosphere where they will not be enticed by the pleasures of the world, the joys of the world, the intoxicating things of the world? Do you understand? No wine, no unclean thing. That's clear enough, isn't it? That means we'll need to empty our houses of all that kind of stuff.

Then no razor shall ever come upon his head. That means you must have an exercise about separation from the time he is born. Now please don't misunderstand me, I know the kind of world we live in, I'm a father and a grandfather.

Dear old Robert Chapman said that the way to rear children was to play with them and pray with them. If you play with them and don't pray with them, then I'm sorry for their souls. But if you pray with them and don't play with them, they won't be very old until they will react against it, possibly leave home. You've got to learn to play with them and pray with them. It's quite correct for children to play, isn't it? The Old Testament talks about children going to play in the streets of Jerusalem. The Lord Jesus in the gospels visualizes the children playing funerals and weddings. So you'll have to get a balance in your home between what is legitimate playing in contrast to what are the intoxicating pleasures of the earth. Wisdom in the nest is required.

"Then Manoah intreated the Lord, and said, O my Lord, let the man of God which thou didst send come again unto us, and teach us what we shall do unto the child that shall be born" (Judges 13:8). "And Manoah said, Now let thy words come to pass. How shall we order the child, and how shall we do unto him?" (verse 12). I think I prefer the Revised Version here; it goes this way: "And Manoah said, Now let thy words come to pass. What shall be the manner of the child and what shall be his work?"

First of all I want you to notice carefully that having received this promise of God, Manoah takes it for granted that what God had promised He was able to perform. In this Manoah and his wife stand in contradistinction to other persons in the Word of God. Remember that Sarah was a barren woman and when the Lord revealed to Abraham (and Sarah was behind him in the tent) that Sarah would have a son, she laughed in unbelief. The Lord said, "Wherefore did Sarah laugh?" Laughing at the impossibility of a woman of her age, who had been barren all her life, bearing a child. In the New Testament scriptures in the opening chapters of the gospel of Luke, you have a priest characterised by unbelief. In contradistinction you have the blessing of Mary, the mother of the Lord Jesus, "Blessed is she that believed." Here in this chapter Manoah and his wife stand in the same rank as Mary and in the same rank as Hannah, who in these impossible circumstances did not doubt for one moment the promise of God. Said Manoah, "Teach us what we shall do with the child that shall be born." He grasped by faith the promise of God. That is real faith: it is to believe God.

When I think of this chapter, I think of Abraham who is very similar. Romans chapter 4 builds the truth of justification upon the incident in Abraham's life where God promised him a child. I read that when God made promise to Abraham that out of his loins through Sarah there would be a son born, Abraham considered well the deadness of his own body and considered well the deadness of Sarah's womb and he said, "Impossible!" Then my Bible says, "He staggered not, but believed God." He just believed what God said, he hadn't a doubt. He believed God, and I read that "his faith was reckoned for righteousness." "Now," says the Spirit of God, "it was not written for his sake alone, that it was imputed to him; but for us also, to whom it shall be imputed, if we believe on him that raised up Jesus our Lord from the dead; who was delivered for our offences, and was raised again for our justification." What is that telling me? It is telling me that the saving faith of the New Testament is identical with the faith which Abraham exercised in the Old Testament. Abraham believed God. I just believe God.

How did Abraham believe God? He believed God this way: he considered the state of death, and he believed that God would bring a living son out of a state of death. He just believed God. God said, Abraham, you've done that, I'll reckon you righteous: in other words, I'll forgive all your sins. God adds, It is not written for Abraham alone but for us who have believed on Him (God) who raised up Jesus our Lord from the dead. What did Abraham believe? He believed that God would bring a living son out of the state of death. What do I believe? What do you believe? You believe, do you not, that God brought a living Son out of the state of death? With Abraham it was a dead womb; for you and I it is an empty tomb! God brought a living son, Isaac, out of a dead womb. Abraham believed God: that's how he was justified. You and I believe that God has brought a living Son, Christ, out of a state of death. Who was that living Son? He who was delivered for our offences: He died for me. Raised again because of my justification: He has risen for me. How did I come into the good of it? I just believed God! How do I know it? God said it.

Manoah did believe God, didn't he? You will notice he showed he believed God in this way, that he said, "Teach us what we shall do to the child that shall be born." He wanted divine guidance relative to the child that should be born — teach us what to do. You'll notice his second request was, What type of child shall the child be? what is the manner of the child? His third request was, And how shall we do unto him? or, What shall be his work? I suppose that is a problem that should face every young Christian couple. It is a problem that should face every young Christian that has an exercise to be married and rear a family for God — "what shall we do unto the child?" How do we bring him up? I know when we had our first child we got a book, I think it was given to my wife while she was still in hospital, and I can guarantee that we carried it out to the very letter. The rest of our children came up by rule of thumb and they did just as well. But young folks seem very concerned as to how to bring up their children; that was the problem here: how? And so there is a need for a deep exercise, asking the Lord not how to bring up our children physically, but how to bring up our children spiritually for God. That is what they wanted. "Teach us what shall be done unto the child that shall be born." Of course, they had already received, in a measure, instructions: no wine, no strong drink, no razor upon his head. They were to circle that child around with a deep spiritual interest as well as a deep natural interest, and preserve that child from every influence that would deflect him in any way from a path of life-time Nazariteship for God.

The next question is "What shall be the manner of the child?" What type shall the child be? what talents shall the child have? what will be his bent in life? if you like. That's a problem for young parents. As our children begin to grow up we wonder whether they will take this course, or that course in life. Then ultimately, what will be his work? I want to spiritualise that for you, my dear young Christian, it is no use talking to grandfathers and grandmothers about this. But, young Christians, if God should put into your hands in days to come little children to rear for Himself, there is a need for a deep exercise that you might be able to shape that child in character to be something for God. To direct that child in order that he or she might have desires early after salvation. Then having brought that child to Christ, try to develop desires to spend time with God and time over the reading of the Scriptures: and you should be looking forward and saying to yourself, Just what has God fitted that child to be?

One perturbing thing is that young parents in these days give a lot of thought to what their children are going to be, but it is generally what they are going to be in this world, and they forget about the next. What profession, what job, what trade are they going to fill in this world? But how about what they are going to be for God? what they are going to be in the assembly? what about their Christian character, their Christian service? These, my dear young Christians, are the primary things in life. When you are getting on in years it doesn't matter whether your children are professors or dustmen. What really does matter in life is what that child of yours is for God. Somebody's child could be holding down a top educational post, and still be unsaved. What's the good of that? Somebody could be holding down a top job in the medical profession, has made a profession, but you never hear his voice in the meeting and he never does a single thing for God: he comes and goes, and is silent and helpless in divine things. Tell me what profit is there in that? We are only passing through, we are only pilgrims going home, and the little time we are here is our education for positions in the administration of the Kingdom. A man can be a professor here, but if he is nothing for God he will be very inferior in the Kingdom.

Would you rather your children have a top position in the future administration, or a top position in some profession in this life? Dear young Christian, think it out! That little child that God will put into your hands will not only live for time but for eternity, and the first thing is being saved. The second thing: train them for positions of administration in the Kingdom. You only train for positions in the Kingdom by developing Christian character, by growing in the things of God, and becoming useful in the assembly and in the service of God. The measure of their fidelity down here in this life will be the measure of their position in the administration of the Kingdom.

How we need, don't we, to get our eyes off earth level; how we need to get our eyes on the future, on the world to come, when we are thinking of our own families. Let me repeat, position here may be important, they've got to get through, they've got to live, it's a difficult busy world: but the thing that is of primary importance in the rearing of young families for God today is what they are going to be for God and for eternity. Let's all write it upon our souls.

Think now of this boy Samson being born into this particular home. I know he's not born until almost the last verse of the chapter, but his nest is being prepared.

There is no wine, no strong drink, no unclean thing. Everything is ready. But there are two things the Spirit of God seems to add to that home, and these are two things that are essential in every Christian home. You say, what are these two things? There was a sacrifice, and I judge that the smell of that sacrifice was never forgotten in that home, it was never forgotten by those parents; for on the day that the angel of the Lord appeared to Manoah and his wife for the second time they made an offering. Made an offering under divine instructions: a burnt offering and a meal offering. They brought the burnt offering, and there it was placed before Jehovah, and I read, "So Manoah took a kid [that's a burnt offering] with a meal offering, and offered it upon a rock unto the Lord: and the angel did wondrously." Now the angel here is, of course, the angel of the Lord, the angel is a Christophany, the angel is the One whose name is "Wonderful". So you have the Lord Jesus doing something wonderful. Where is he? Upon the rock. You read, "That Rock was Christ." So that is the second emphasis on the Person of Christ. Then you have the burnt offering aspect of the death of Christ which is primarily for the glory of God, a sacrifice of devotion to God Himself. Associated with that is a meal offering which speaks of the moral excellency of the Lord Jesus throughout His life. The meal offering is never offered without a burnt offering. So you have the preciousness of the life of Christ associated with the preciousness of the death of Christ, and there they are offered in sacrifice to God. The New Testament scriptures state of the Lord Jesus: "who through the eternal Spirit offered himself without spot to God."

When Manoah and his wife offered these things upon

a rock, a flame went up toward heaven from the altar. I read, "When the flame went up toward heaven from off the altar, the angel of the Lord ascended in the flame of the altar." So to quote an old hymn, which some people don't like, we could say,

> "I've been to the altar and witnessed the lamb,
>   Burnt wholly to ashes for me,
> Watched its sweet savour ascending on high,
>   Accepted, O Father, by Thee."

This is what Manoah and his wife did: they gazed upon the sacrifice and smelled its lovely fragrance. In other words, they looked upon and they breathed in deeply of the sacrifice of Calvary in its most precious aspect. Here is a father and mother who waited in that home for that child to be born, and fresh in their nostrils was the smell of a sacrifice they would never forget. More than that: as they watched that sacrifice they saw it lit, no doubt, by divine flame and they watched the angel of the Lord go up in the flame of the altar.

Turn in your mind to the New Testament scriptures, and think not only of the burnt offering aspect of the death of Christ but that the Lord Jesus having offered Himself through the eternal Spirit without spot to God, makes His way out to Bethany. Standing with Him on Olivet's slopes there are the eleven. There around Him are His own, and as they watch they see Him gradually go up. Pictured in our chapter He goes up in the flame of the altar, an indication of Heaven's acceptance of the sacrifice. Divided into two events in our New Testament scriptures, seen as one event in our chapter: the sacrifice, and then the angel of the Lord going up in the flame of the altar. I turn to Calvary and I see the Sacrifice. I turn to the Mount of Olives and I see the One who is the accepted sacrifice going up, as it were, in the flame of the altar. Think of the amazement of those parents as they realised that this One who they wanted to entertain was none other than the angel of God and they watch him do wondrously at the place of sacrifice.

Christian parents, have we not had that experience in our lives? how often have we been to Calvary and seen God doing wondrously? Notice that text: "He [Deity] through the eternal Spirit [Deity] offered himself without spot to God." Calvary is the operation of divine Persons. "He", you say, is the Lord Jesus; yes, but He is God manifest in flesh. "Through the eternal Spirit": yes, He is the Spirit of God. "Offered himself without spot to God": God in Heaven, God in His holiness. Redemption was accomplished entirely by divine Persons. The work of atonement is the accomplishment of the Trinity. Look to Calvary and you will see the One whose name is Wonderful doing wondrously. How often, my dear fellow Christian, have you and I acknowledged that Calvary is so wonderful we can never, never fully grasp all that happened there?

Then we have not only been to Calvary, but we've been to the Mount of the Ascension. Have we not seen Him go up? Oh! it would have been grand to have been on earth when He actually went up: to be gathered around the person of the Lord Jesus and realise suddenly that He was gradually going up. No! He didn't go up in a flash, He went gradually. Everything to do with the ascension of Christ is gradual. If He had gone up in a flash He would have vanished out of their sight, there would have been no proof of the ascension; but they

watched a Man in a real body being carried up, taken
up, received up. As He goes up those dear disciples had
the sublime privilege of seeing that body ascend until all
they could see was the palms of two pierced hands and
the sandals upon two pierced feet. They saw Him go up!
Then I read, "They returned to Jerusalem." Would
they ever forget Calvary? Would they ever forget the last
sight they had of the ascending Christ before the glory
wrapped Him in?

If that be true in the New Testament it must be true of
Manoah and his wife as first they smelled the sacrifice,
watched while the Angel of the Lord did wondrously,
then saw Him go up in the flame of the altar. This
privileged boy was born into that home where godly
parents had stripped it of the world's intoxications,
stripped it of all the world's uncleanness. Godly parents
had done all they could to shelter this child from all
defiling influences. But please, that is all negative, and I
trust, my dear brother, dear sister, that your home is not
a negative home. So much Christianity is negative: it is
what we don't enjoy, what we don't do, what we don't
allow. Ah! but while they had put out the world's
intoxication, the world's uncleanness, and godly hands
were sheltering that home, there was in that home
something that was heavenly and delightful: there was a
constant remembrance of the smell of a sacrifice and a
constant remembrance of a Man who had gone up in the
flame of the altar. My dear brethren and sisters, as we
think of our own homes, are they negative homes or
positive homes? Are our homes places where you smell
constantly the fragrance of the sacrifice of Christ
enjoyed in our souls, there for fellow Christians to smell
with us, there for the members of our own family? They

are not to be occupied with negatives, but to be entranced with the fragrance of the Person and sacrifice of Christ. So while there are many things we won't have in our homes, are our children conscious that we are men and women who have never lost the sight of a Man going up in the flame of the altar?

The New Testament talks about it: "Ye died with Christ" (Col. 2:20); "If ye then be raised with Christ, ... set your mind on things above, not on things on the earth" (Col. 3:1,2) ... things in Heaven, where Christ is seated on the right hand of God. The Colossian Christians looked back to the smell of a sacrifice, and they looked up at the Man who had gone up in the flame of the altar. My dear young Christian, if you've been reared in a home like that, you've something to thank God for. The fragrance of a sacrifice and the sight of a Man in the glory enriching the atmosphere in which you were reared.

This child was born in an ideal atmosphere. I do not know if his home was rich or poor, I don't know if it was well furnished or not, whether it was comfortable or uncomfortable. The home I was reared in was very uncomfortable, but I tell you there was the smell of a sacrifice, there was the sight of a Man gone up. However humble our homes may be, whatever we have, or don't have, of this world's goods, these things are essential —the fragrance of Calvary and the remembrance of a Man who has gone up in the flame of the altar. After the child was born and after the passage of years, it says, "The child grew, and the Lord blessed him. And the Spirit of the Lord began to move him." That's lovely! It's lovely when our children are born, isn't it? It's lovely to see them grow, it's lovely to see them born again, it's

lovely to see them growing spiritually. It's a great thrill
when the Spirit of God begins to move them. When you
see that boy of yours talking to his school pals about the
Saviour, quite thrilled if he can get somebody along to
the meeting. The first signs of a desire to do something
for the Lord — the Spirit of God begins to move them.

With some of us who were reared in Christian homes
it didn't make a lot of difference getting saved. We
cannot tell you how many times we were drunk; for we
never were. Or how many times we played billiards; for
we never did. Or how immoral we were; we didn't know
anything about that. We got saved. Well, what evidence
was there in our lives that we were saved? Simply this,
that the Spirit of God began to move us, we began to
want to do things to please the Lord, to tell others about
the Saviour and introduce others to Christ. These were
the evidences of new life. Is there a young Christian here
not long saved: any evidence of new life yet? Oh I know
you had a bad temper and you can have that even
though reared in a Christian home, being saved changes
that. I know if you have been characterised by
selfishness, being saved changes that. I know that being
saved makes you willing to help in every way you
possibly can. These are evidences of being saved. Here
the Spirit of God began to move him and these were the
very earliest evidences of this child of promise who had
been sheltered by godly parents and reared in such a
home.

Consider, too, that the Spirit of God began to move
him between Zorah and Eshtaol. I like that: the Spirit of
God began to move him at home. That's the place
where conversion makes a difference. Sometimes I go to
a home and the parents will tell me, their son or

daughter has a Sunday school class and is getting on alright in the meeting, but they're not very helpful at home: still bad-tempered, lacking in co-operation with their parents, wanting to be at the meeting but leaving mother to do all the washing-up. The traits of Christianity mean that if you want to get to the meeting your mother wants to get there too, so you will do everything you can to make sure she will get there. At home the Spirit of God began to move him. A selfish young woman or a selfish young man will become a helpful young woman or man when the Spirit of God begins to move.

Let me speak again to you young folk. The Spirit of God began to move him. Where? On his own doorstep. I wonder if that should be written on our souls these days? I wonder if you have ever stood and preached in your own street, my brother? I tell you, it takes some doing. The first time I did it in Scotland, as a young married man, I stood almost outside my own door to preach the gospel. If you are not able to preach the gospel on your own doorstep, you are not really fit to preach it anywhere else: that's the place of your public testimony. Remember the words of the Saviour, "Go home to your friends and tell what great things the Lord hath done for thee" — the responsibility first of taking the message near home. I find some young men quite prepared to preach the gospel forty miles from home, prepared to go along to another assembly to preach the gospel, but often in their own assembly their voice is never heard in the prayer meeting, or worshipping in the morning meeting. All their activities are outside to build up some other assembly. Please, my dear young brother, your first responsibility is to your own assembly. Maybe we are dissipating our energies and instead of concentrating on building up our own local assembly, we use our energies to build up — things of God, of course — but elsewhere. First of all please — home. In a large assembly you can afford to have your young men going out to preach the gospel: "From you sounded out the Word of God," says the New Testament scriptures. But, young man, never let the home base suffer, never let your home assembly go down while you are being active elsewhere. If things are getting weak at home, well, dig in at home and build up at home. When you've got a sound, solid, prospering home base then you can spread out with the gospel elsewhere, but your responsibility is to do it at home.

Now, with chapter 13 full of such wonderful things as the preparation for this birth and the perfection and development of this young man, the tragedy of the next chapter is a series of "downs". Now look at them: verse 1, "and Samson went down;" verse 5, "then went Samson down;" verse 7, "and he went down;" verse 10, "his father went down." Then there is a little bit of hope at the end of the chapter, verse 19: "and his anger was kindled and he went up." Go to verse 8 of the next chapter and you read again, "and he went down." In verse 13 you read, "and they bound him with two new cords and brought him up." You'll notice that one time he came up because he was angry, but the next time he came up he wasn't responsible, for they carried him up. So you have the history of a man who went down almost until his last breath, and then his brethren went down and brought him up.

It seems strange, doesn't it? What kind of home was he born in? He was born in a home where the parents looked up, they had seen the vision of the angel of God going up in the flame of the sacrifice. Their eyes were up, up, up. Why were their eyes up? They were up because their affections had been attracted to the Man who did wondrously at a sacrifice and now He had gone up. Their hearts were entwined around Him. My dear young Christian, if you have been reared in a home like that, what a tragedy if your life should be a repetition of Samson's.

I suppose lots of us parents face that situation. It's one thing to see them saved, it's a great thing to see them going on with God. But the next problem in life is: who are they going to marry? for the object that attracts their affection will be the object that shapes their lives for good or for bad. This boy couldn't have had a better background and he couldn't have made a better start, everything was in his favour until there passed by a daughter of the Philistines. You'll notice that it says, "He went down to Timnath, and saw." It's not that he saw and went down, but he went down and saw. In other words, now he has grown he's beginning to take action on his own, and he takes a stroll in Philistine territory. Zorah and Eshtaol are border country, so he takes a stroll into Philistine territory and finds a lovely figure and a pretty face that attracts him. Abraham had a borderland experience when he got away from the altar and he didn't need a tent. He went into the south country where there was a famine and he went down to Egypt. Had he been by his altar you might have heard him say he would call on the name of the Lord. But he got into borderland and he went down.

Samson got into borderland. I want to ask you, my dear young Christian, are you in borderland? You say,

13

What is that? Well, in borderland the smell of the sacrifice isn't so strong — getting away from Calvary, from the debt you owe the Saviour. In borderland he was away from the folk who had a perpetual vision of the Man who had gone up in the flame of the altar, away from the fact that Christ is on high and our affections must be there. He had moved away from the enjoyment of those things towards the Philistines. Young Christians, have you ever been there? Calvary isn't so precious to you as it is to your parents, isn't so precious to you as once it was; and the Man in the glory doesn't seem so real to you as he used to be. You've got into border country! That's when you get colder towards the Saviour and you get a little bit nearer to the world; it doesn't seem as hostile to you as it used to do; you feel a little bit more at home there: and somehow you don't feel as happy in the presence of God as you once did —borderland! And it is when you get into borderland that the attraction of the Philistines seems to be so impressive.

My dear young Christian, if you want to be kept, keep near Calvary. If you want to be kept, keep your eye on an ascended Christ. Says the New Testament, "Keep yourselves in the love of God." Perpetually occupy yourself with the loveliness of Christ in His life, in His sacrifice and in His glory, and that will keep you from getting into borderland. Keep you from finding a place in your heart for something or someone that is foreign to Christ. Remember please, **he went down**.

Notice, with Samson it was a matter of affection, an affection that governed the direction in which he went. He saw a woman of Timnath and then he said, "She pleaseth me well." The path of association with the woman of Timnath was, firstly, his affections were entwined around her, and instead of her attracting him up, she attracted him down. Solemn, isn't it? I think it is all the more bitter because they saw the Spirit of God begin to move him, and after the Spirit of God had begun to move him there came before him a young woman of Timnath. He went down! It's a joy to every parent as they see their boy or girl beginning to be moved by the Spirit of God. But then there flits across their vision a young man or a young woman who is a Philistine, not saved, and their affections are drawn away from the Man of the altar and their sight is drawn away from the Man who has gone up in the flame of the altar. Their affections become entwined around an object of the world, and they go down.

Let me show you this, that when young Christians go down from Christian homes, you have a very pathetic thing here. He saw the daughters of the women of Timnath and he told his father and his mother; that's interesting. Trace the word "told" in this man's life: it seems almost that in a kind of simplicity, when he allowed his affections to go out to a Philistine, he told his father and his mother, as though he thought they would be pleased. Of course, they were parents that believed that an unequal yoke was wrong and so they talked straight to him. Verse 6, notice please, now he is on the road down into the Philistines land to meet the girl he has seen and the end of the verse says, "And he told not his father or his mother." You see, my dear young Christian, if, like Samson, you allow yourself to take steps towards a Philistine partner in a Philistine world, at first you may feel free to discuss it with your parents, but when they don't agree, the thing becomes secretive.

It causes estrangement between you and the parents you love. I guess that's absolutely true to life, isn't it? Young Christians grow up with Christian parents, they set their affections on someone who is not saved, their parents don't approve, and from that point onwards they become secretive and act in defiance of their parents.

Notice please, the next step: verse 17, "He told her." First, he told his parents. Then, he did not tell his father and mother. He becomes secretive and doesn't reveal to them what he is doing. But now he is beginning to open out to the girl, and he's telling her, not his parents. Notice the development of that. Go to chapter 16 verse 17, "And he told her." This was another Philistine woman, and he's telling her. He is completely removed from his parents now! The confidence and the fellowship he once had with them is severed, and he is opening his heart to Philistines: he tells his first wife, and then he tells Delilah. What is the result? Within a short period he has lost his Nazariteship, his eyes and his liberty. Philistines, my dear young Christian, will drag you away from confidence and fellowship with your parents, they will entice you from that until you will feel more at home with Philistines than you do with your parents and the saints; and you'll find that Philistines become your confidants. In the end, Philistines will rob you completely of all you ever were for God and leave you blinded, in bondage, wretched and miserable. Watch the Philistines!

Let me put it this way. My dear young Christian, if your affections have gone out to a girl or a fellow and you don't feel happy talking to your parents about it, you had better break off the friendship. For that is a Philistine friendship when you feel free to tell that girl or boy or their family something you have a conscience about mentioning to your own Christian parents.

We have already mentioned the tragedy that this man, born in a house where parents were constantly looking up, that he should be characterised by "going down". I want you to notice that when he went down **he saw**. Further down the chapter we read that he went down again and **he spoke** to the young woman whom he had seen down in the land of the Philistines. I read again that **she pleased him well**.

It would be wise to take time to examine carefully the constant repetition of DOWN in the remainder of the record of this man's life.

"And Samson went down to Timnath, and saw a woman of Timnath of the daughters of the Philistines."
(14:1)

"Then went Samson down, and his father and mother." (14:5)

"He went down and talked to the woman." (14:7)

"So his father went down unto the woman, and Samson made there a feast." (14:10)

"He went down to Ashkelon." (14:19)

"And he smote them hip and thigh with a great slaughter, and went down and dwelt in the top of the rock Etam." (15:8)

"But the Philistines took him and put out his eyes, and brought him down to Gaza." (16:21)

"Then his brethren and all the house of his father came down, and took him and brought him up." (16:31)

Standing out on the surface, of course, is the warning of the danger of going down, the danger of going down into Philistine country. Please let us remember this is not Moabite country, this is God's land. This is not the world of gross iniquity, of violence and sin; this is the world of religion and culture. It's the world of religion that takes the name of God and Christ — that is the Philistine world. What a danger there is today of our young people going down into Philistine country. Many of them, reared as they are, would not dream of going down into a Moab world, would not dream of Moab associations; but the cultured and the religious, the people who, shall we say, live almost on the border of divine things and are not so much opposed thereto; not saved but quite considerate when you express your sentiments relative to religion: these people may attract. But they are Philistines!

It is possible for our young men to see a woman in the Philistines' land, to talk to her, and to find that possible worldly partners are pleasant to look at and pleasant to talk to. Have you young men ever found that? Young women: religious, respectable, refined, pleasant! There is always a danger in looking upon a member of the opposite sex when he or she is fair, and the only thing you are thinking about is the way he or she looks and speaks; you are not considering what the mind of God is in the matter at all. That is the main mistake that Samson makes in Judges chapter 14. He went down, and he saw; he went down, and he talked to; and her face was so attractive and her voice was so charming that it wasn't very long before she had won a place in his heart.

The first thing of course is not to go down to Philistine country, to avoid Philistine country, to avoid Philistine associations. Oh, you have to rub shoulders with them in business! and I suppose it is better to be in business with those kind of folk than with the Moab type. But in your social movements, in your evenings and your holidays, wherever you may go, avoid Philistines. For if you avoid Philistines you'll neither see their charms, nor be moved by their voices.

One thing I remember a dear brother in England saying on one occasion was, that he considered it was absolutely essential for young men and women, long before they ever fell in love, to solemnly before God determine never to allow their affections to go out to somebody who is not saved. I think that is a good point, I think he has got something there. You see, once you have seen a charming Philistine face and listened to a charming Philistine voice, the battle is lost; you are already enticed. It is a case of determining, in the fear of God, that however charming a face you may see, or however charming a voice you might hear, that you will not allow them to draw you away from absolute fidelity to Christ.

That charming face, shall we say, was a satanic attraction to take the deliverer of Israel into the bondage of love in Philistinia before he was ever bound by the Philistines and lost his sight. First of all it was bands of love that held him but in the end, robbed of his Nazarite character, a prison held him! But the first thing was his affection to a Philistine woman. So, my dear young Christian, the Bible says, "Keep thy heart with all diligence." Put a guard around your affections, determinedly keep your heart; lest, in spite of making a good beginning in divine things, you find your heart ensnared.

Have you noticed that there did exist, at the beginning of the chapter, an excellent relationship between this young man and his father and mother? But we have pointed out before that when this young woman came into his life, gradually the lovely intimate relationship that existed between parents and son was broken.

Notice in the following verses the estrangement between Samson and his parents gradually developing, and along with it his gradual envelopment by the world.

"He told his father and his mother."			(14:2)

"But he told not his father or his mother."		(14:6)

"He told them not that he had taken the honey."
							(14:9)

"I have not told my father nor my mother, and shall I tell it thee?"					(14:16)

"He told her, and she told the riddle to the children of her people."					(14:17)

"Tell me, I pray thee, wherein thy great strength lieth."						(16:6)

"Now tell me, I pray thee, wherewith thou mightest be bound."						(16:10)

"Hitherto thou hast mocked me and told me lies: tell me wherewith thou mightest be bound."		(16:13)

"Thou hast not told me wherein thy great strength lieth."						(16:15)

"She pressed him daily with her words, and urged him, so that his soul was vexed unto death. Then he told her all his heart."					(16:16,17)

My dear young Christian, you may have had the sublime privilege of being reared in a Christian home, and up to the moment you have shared everything with your parents: your interests, even in the members of the opposite sex, your interests in life, your desires to serve the Lord; and you have enjoyed that happy fellowship of oneness. I tell you, if you allow a Philistine to come into your life, gradually that intimate confiding the one with the other will be strained. There will be a pull between your parents and that Philistine friend, and gradually your affinity to your parents will break and the affinity will become stronger with the Philistine. Broken-hearted parents will see you gradually enticed away. You say, Impossible! you don't know the relationship that exists between my parents and myself.

If you go into Philistine country like Samson and you see a Philistine person of the opposite sex as he did, and are charmed by a face, charmed by a voice, the nearer you get to that Philistine the further away you'll get from your godly parents. It is also true that, the nearer you get to that Philistine, the further you'll get from God. It's one of the unalterable principles, and you won't be the exception! He told his father and mother; and I was going to say, almost innocently, naively. Why didn't he know it was wrong to marry a Philistine? — he had been a Nazarite from his birth. What does it mean to be a Nazarite? It means to be separate from everything that is not of God. He comes home so simply, almost as though it was the right thing to do, and says, "Mother, I'm thinking about marrying a Philistine. Would you and father make arrangements for the marriage?" What he was suggesting — maybe he didn't understand — was the negation of the whole of his Nazariteship. We'll talk about that for a minute or two.

"A vow of a Nazarite, to separate himself unto the Lord: he shall separate himself from wine and strong drink, and shall drink no vinegar of wine, or vinegar of strong drink, neither shall he drink any liquor of grapes, nor eat moist grapes or dried. All the days of his separation shall he eat nothing that is made of the vine tree, from the kernels even to the husk. All the days of his separation shall no razor come upon his head ... All the days that he separateth himself unto the Lord he shall come at no dead body." (Numbers 6:1-6.)

Here was a man with long hair. It's a shame for a man to have long hair, but this man had taken the place of shame for the whole of his life under divine instructions. Why? Because he was to be a Nazarite from his mother's womb, he was to be separate all his life. His Nazariteship demanded, of course, separation from everybody that was not of God; his separation from wine and from everything that was unclean. A strange man: the first thing I find is that he falls in love with a woman who didn't know God. That was a breaking of Nazariteship. The second thing: he finds himself in a vineyard. You'll say he wasn't drinking wine neither was he eating grapes, but why was he in a vineyard? He's getting as near to the thing as he possibly can! Some Christians are like that: they run as near to sin as they possibly can. What was he doing on one occasion? He took honey out of the dead carcase of a lion, then he slew a multitude of men with the jawbone of an ass that he wasn't supposed to touch — an unclean thing. Yet all the while his hair was long, proclaiming to everyone, "I'm a Nazarite." Yet he was neither a Nazarite in being separate from Philistines, nor in not being near the vine, nor in not touching anything unclean. In other words he had the external sign, but he did not have the reality.

You and I have been through the waters of baptism. We would say, rightly, that baptism is associated with conversion; if that were carried out there wouldn't be any applicants for assembly fellowship who were not baptised. That means that everybody who is received into assembly fellowship should be baptised. We all believe that, we've got the ceremony. Samson had the ceremony. But how about the moral teaching? He hadn't got that. You and I may have the ceremony of baptism. What about its moral teaching? It is possible to be ceremonially baptised in water and never have the moral teaching. Do you think Samson's long hair had any virtue before God when he wasn't living a separated life? Has baptism lost its value if we do not morally live out the truth of it? I'm not saying you shouldn't be baptised; you should. But baptism is a ceremony that must be associated with a moral condition. My dear fellow-believer, have we the ceremony without the condition?

Again, all our sisters are sitting here with their heads covered — yes, the Word of God teaches it, there is no doubt about it. The doctrine of headship is clear in God's Word. And because angels saw Lucifer revolting against headship, and because angels knew that Eve revolted against headship, angels behold in our gatherings sisters with their heads covered, and they see one sphere where there has not been a revolt against headship. That's why our sisters have their heads covered — not because of the brethren, but because of the angels. Here is a sphere where angels see the acknowledgement of headship. That's the ceremony. What about the moral condition? My dear sister, do you acknowledge headship? are you subject to your husband and to the elders of the assembly? If, my dear sister, you are not, you have the ceremony but not the moral correspondence. For there is a moral correspondence of subjection.

Samson's father and mother wisely said to him, "Is there never a woman among the daughters of thy brethren, or among all my people, that thou goest to take a wife of the uncircumcised Philistines?" Any godly parents would speak to their sons like that, and they would have every reason so to do because there are such a number of excellent Christian young women, so much out of proportion to the number of available young men. So this verse is very appropriate to any unattached young man: "Is there never a woman among the daughters of thy brethren and among all my people?" There is never any excuse whatsoever for any Christian young man in an assembly marrying an unsaved girl.

It's not the same for young women. I couldn't use these exact words, because sometimes there is not a man among the sons of thy brethren and among all my people: so some of our young sisters may be in the unfortunate position where there is not available a young man who knows the Lord. No excuse! The Word of God is still perfectly clear: "Be ye not unequally yoked together with unbelievers." If you dare, my dear young sister, to disobey the Word of God, let me tell you plainly, you will be in for a life of sorrow. You will live to regret the step that you have taken. I said you will! Revelation chapter 2: the Lord sends a message to a church at Pergamos which means "a marriage objected to." Unequal yokes are marriages that Heaven objects to. If God objects to your marriage, I tell you He will not bless it. Don't marry an unconverted person and then ask God to bless it. Don't marry an unsaved partner and then have the audacity to get down on your knees and ask God to save him or her. In obedience to the Word of God, even if you are a young woman and there are no young men about, you must bow implicitly to the Word of God. Remember this, that when you stand before the Judgment Seat of Christ there will be abundant reward for all our sisters who have remained single when they could have been married; have remained single in obedience to the Word of God. I become more and more convinced that at the Judgment Seat of Christ there is going to be more reward for obedience to God's Word than for a multiplicity of service. We have developed an idea of recent years that it is only our service to the Lord that's going to be commended at the Judgment Seat of Christ. I submit to you that our service to the Lord —what we generally call service — will take a very minor place at the Judgment Seat of Christ, and our moral character and obedience to the will of God and the measure in which we have pleased the Lord are the things that will be commended.

Let us notice that his father and his mother gave the girl the right name. I don't think Samson would be very pleased at their description of the young woman he wanted to marry. They called her the daughter of an uncircumcised Philistine. Do you young folks ever get annoyed with your parents? — I suppose you do. When they make some caustic remark about that unsaved girl or unsaved fellow you are setting your eyes on, don't be surprised! Manoah and his wife weren't too complimentary about this young woman. They gave her the right name: she was of the uncircumcised. To a Jew that was obnoxious: no sign of the covenant, no connection with God. A Philistine — a person that took the name of God's land but didn't know God. Maybe if your parents

give that unsaved friend of yours the right name they
will say, You know they are not saved, they have no
interest in divine things, they have no covenant with the
blood of sacrifice, and are religious but do not know the
Lord. Many an unconverted man would like to have for
a wife one of our godly young sisters! There is many an
unconverted girl who may make a false profession in
order to get one of our godly young men! Our young
sisters are of such an excellent character, and our
converted young men are so upright, they would make
excellent partners.

In spite, however, of the way the parents talked about
this young women, Samson said unto his father, "Get
her for me, for she pleaseth me well." Now, my dear
young Christian, you can please yourself, you can please
your parents, or you can please the Lord. I could add,
you could please the Devil, but should I be as unkind as
that? Bring it down to this: you can please yourself or
please the Lord. I suppose the matter of whom you are
going to marry is a matter that, naturally speaking,
belongs to yourself. Whatever your parents say, you'll
say, "I'll go my own way." So it comes down to this: it's
a question of whether you are going to please the Lord or
please yourself. Twice over we read "She pleaseth me
well."

I have been asked sometimes, What does it mean
when it says, "But his father and his mother knew not
that it was of the Lord, that he sought an occasion
against the Philistines: for at that time the Philistines
had dominion over Israel"? You know that God is the
only One who can bring good out of evil. It could never
be the mind of God that the man who was to deliver
God's people from the Philistines should marry a

Philistine. That would be a contradiction of terms. God had raised him up "that he should begin to deliver Israel." But instead of delivering Israel from the Philistines, he was contemplating marrying, going into bondage to a Philistine. Then I read, "It was of the Lord." Why? When I consider the previous judges, some of them made tragic mistakes, but they did know who the enemy was they ought to fight. Othniel knew who the enemy was, Ehud knew who the enemy was, Gideon knew who the enemy was. Jephthah knew, when he was raised up, who the enemy was. They had no doubts. You don't find them compromising with the enemy. But this man, did he not know who the enemy was? Instead of sharpening his sword, or getting his ox-goad, or a tent-peg, he seems to forget that he had been raised up to be a warrior and he goes for a walk and falls in love with the enemy. God — seeing the type of man that he was, who would not fight the enemy unless he had to — God will now turn that out so that he finds himself in a series of circumstances where he's slaying Philistines, but never once does he appear to slay Philistines because he realised God had sent him to do it. He slew Philistines (1) because they guessed his riddle and (2) because they burned his wife and her father. In the end why did he slay Philistines? He says, "That I may be avenged for my two eyes."

He never said, Lord, help me to slay the Philistines because they are thine enemies, or the enemies of the people of God, holding them down in bondage. No! that wasn't his idea in slaying Philistines at all. He's slaying Philistines because they are after him, but he was slaying Philistines. So, God overruled the tendency of this man to get linked up affectionately with Philistines, to bring

him into circumstances where he slew them: just for his
own self-defence and in order that he might wreak
vengeance upon his enemies. What does it say? "But his
father and his mother knew not that it was of the Lord,
(would be overruled of the Lord) ... for God was seeking
an occasion against the Philistines."

Verse 5 says "Samson went down, and his father and
his mother." That's a problem. Samson went down; he
was wrong. Fell in love with a young woman; that was
wrong. He came home and told his father and mother,
and they told him he was wrong. But watch the next
step: the next step is that his father and mother go down.
His father and mother are now obligated to go down to a
place where they should not have been. Why? Because
he first went down, fell in love with somebody that was
down, then he got interested in going down. Finally,
determined on marriage, his father and mother were
obligated to go down. Many Christian parents have
found themselves in a similar situation, because their
sons or their daughters have entered into affectionate
relationships with an unconverted partner, they have
found themselves in that awful position where they have
had to say, Well now, shall I boycott the wedding or
shall I go to the wedding? Shall I refuse to have anything
to do with the wedding, or shall I compromise to give
her a good wedding and try and get through it as
happily as I can, realising that an unequal yoke is
contrary to the will of God?

Dear young Christian, think soberly of the heart-rend
your parents will have if you ever suggest marrying
somebody who is not saved. Oh, I'm not saying what the
parents should do; I wouldn't dare. In the mercy of God
I've never been in that situation. I don't know what I'd

do, if my heart were torn between doing the best for my daughter and fidelity to God and His word. That was the dilemma Manoah and his wife found themselves in. I'm not going to condemn them; they went down. I wonder how they felt if, as I suppose, they were present at the wedding ceremony and they saw their son who was a Nazarite joined in holy matrimony to a Philistine. If you can imagine what they felt like, see that you don't repeat those tragic circumstances in your own life.

Consider, that having gone down and done certain things that, as a Nazarite, he should not have done, on two occasions he deceives his parents. He deceives them on the subject of Nazariteship. I read "Then went Samson down and his father and his mother to Timnath, and came to the vineyards of Timnath." Think of that. Not only was he in the vineyards, his mother was in the vineyards. She had been told to touch not wine or strong drink; and while it doesn't say they were drinking, it was borderland. Is it possible that your parents might defile their consciences, my dear young Christian, by something you do? Notice please, a young lion roared against him: that should have made him think. Oh! Samson's not a picture of Christ, not here, no, no! Samson was going down and a young lion roared against him, a young lion, a picture of the devil. A young lion opposing a man going down. Have you ever taken a path down and heard the lion roar against you, the opposition roaring against you? God allows the roar of the lion to make him stop and think on the path of **going down.**

"The Spirit of the Lord came mightily upon him" (verse 6). What for? Well, to deliver him from the young lion. To kill Philistines? No, no. To fight the battles of
14

the Lord? No, no. Just to extricate him from the difficulty he found himself in by going down. If he had obeyed the will of God he would never have been there. Verse 19: "And the Spirit of the Lord came upon him." Why? He had been clever and made up a riddle and put it like a piece of poetry. Notice that riddles and poetry are one of the features of Samson's life. You have poetry in verse 18, and in chapter 15 verse 16 you have more poetry about the jawbone of an ass. Going back to verse 14, "Out of the eater came forth meat, and out of the strong came forth sweetness." The Philistine young men obtained the answer to his riddle through the betrayal by his Philistine wife. The Spirit of the Lord came upon him, not to fight the battles of the Lord, but to avenge himself because he had lost his riddle.

Notice carefully the mentions of the Spirit of God in the life of Samson:

"And the Spirit of the Lord came mightily upon him, and he rent him [the young lion] as he would have rent a kid." (14:6)

"And the Spirit of the Lord came upon him, and he went down to Ashkelon, and slew thirty men of them." (14:19)

"The Spirit of the Lord came mightily upon him, and the cords that were upon his arms became as flax that was burnt with fire, and his bands loosed from off his hands." (15:14)

(N.B. The Spirit of God is not mentioned in Samson's life after this. Should we link with this chapter 16:20 "And he wist not that the Lord was departed from him"?)

of the Lord comes upon him. We read of it in chapter 15, verse 14: the tribe of Judah has bound him with ropes and handed him over to the Philistines and "the Spirit of the Lord came mightily upon him." This man was colossal in strength, and on top of his tremendous physical strength the Spirit of the Lord came upon him mightily. A man like that could have destroyed the host of the Philistines, but the only times the Spirit of God comes upon him is to extricate him from difficult circumstances he is found in through disobeying the Word of God. That, not because they were Philistines, but to avenge himself. Samson has seen the power of God in spiritual strength and lives his life so much in folly, that instead of using that power for the glory of God, the only thing he knows of the Spirit of God is being extricated from positions which his folly produced.

Further in verse 6 we read that he rent the lion as he would have rent a kid, "but he told not his father or his mother what he had done." Note that? Then a little later he returns and he finds honey in the carcase of the lion. Verse 9: "And he took thereof in his hands and went on eating, and he came to his father and mother, and he gave them, and they did eat: but he told not them that he had taken the honey out of the carcase of the lion." He didn't tell them. Why was this? He was a Nazarite, he took hold of the lion and he rent it like a kid. It lay there dead, and he was defiled by a dead body; but he didn't tell his father he had broken his Nazariteship. It's very sad when young Christians break their Nazariteship and do not tell their father or their mother. It makes a difference, makes a division, makes for deception. Then he takes honey out of the dead carcase, and that again was the breaking of his

Nazariteship. But there is something else: he took it to
his father and his mother and they did eat. If eating
honey out of a dead carcase defiled Samson, it defiled
them; but he told them not. He would allow his father
and his mother to be defiled, though they didn't know it.

A couple walking holily before the Lord seeking to
obey all His commandments: they became defiled by
eating, but Samson kept them in ignorance of the
matter. What a distance they had descended from the
ceremonial cleanness impressed upon them when the
angel of the Lord appeared first to Manoah's wife!

Eventually Manoah went down and it appears was at
the feast that Samson made, with the thirty companions
— uncircumcised Philistines. Truly he was sitting in the
seat of the scornful (Psalm 1) having fellowship with the
ungodly, those who hate the Lord.

Another feature of Samson's character seems to be an
urge to write snippets of verse on unusual occasions:

"Out of the eater came forth meat,
    And out of the strong came forth sweetness." (14:14)

"If ye had not plowed with my heifer,
    Ye had not found out my riddle."   (14:18)

"With the jawbone of an ass,
    heaps upon heaps,
With the jaw of an ass
    have I slain a thousand men."   (15:16)

While we all remember with gratitude the Psalms of
David expressing depths of emotion and joy in the
various crises of his life, compared with those writings,

Samson's are weak, almost childish, phrases spoken on occasions when strong men would have been galvanised into deeds of valour.

Again he seems to be powerless to control his desire for Philistine women. Why did he always travel in their direction? There was

(a) A woman in Timnath

(b) A harlot in Gaza

(c) A woman in the valley of Sorek — Delilah.

Women who because they were of the uncircumcised Philistines were forbidden to God's people and were unfit partners for a man separated unto God, but were also morally unfit for the affections of any good man. How important that we should heed the instruction: "Keep thy heart with all diligence, for out of it are the issues of life."

Samson had to learn what Philistines were really like at heart. They looked attractive, he enjoyed meeting them and feasting with them. He could put his riddle to them and make his bargain. He could love Delilah, trust her, only to be constantly deceived by her.

He had to learn that while Philistines appear to be friends they would urge a woman to betray her husband, would threaten to burn her and her father if she did not succumb to their wishes. She could weep before Samson in order to get the answer to the riddle. (Beware of the tears of Philistines!) She could press him sore for seven whole days until he told her, and she told the riddle to the children of her people.

The Lord indeed used the occasion against the Philistines, turning Samson's folly to His own glory. "The Spirit of the Lord came upon him, and he went down to Ashkelon, and slew thirty men of them, and took their spoil, and gave change of garments unto them which expounded the riddle. And his anger was kindled, and he went up to his father's house." (Notice "up"). His Philistine father-in-law gave Samson's wife to another Philistine whom Samson had trusted, and had made his companion. This is how Philistines behave. These worldlings who look so attractive are really children of the Devil. So the Lord addressed the Pharisees; and Paul writing in 2 Timothy 3 gives an enlightening description of the characters of those who have a form of godliness but deny the power thereof. Samson learns at great cost. This is not all Philistines will do, for when Samson avenged himself by letting go foxes with firebrands into the standing corn, they came up and burned his wife and her father with fire. "Samson saw a woman in Timnath" ... "The Philistines burned her with fire". What catastrophic events often come upon the ungodly indirectly brought about by the waywardness of the people of God! She and her father burned to death had a real connection with the fact that Samson went down. This sad incident was used in the sovereign ways of God as another occasion against the Philistines: "He smote them hip and thigh with a great slaughter."

Samson had also to endure the treachery of his fellow countrymen, even those of the noble tribe of Judah. Three thousand men of Judah said, "Knowest thou not that the Philistines are rulers over us?" In the days of Ehud he could say, "Follow after me, for the Lord hath delivered your enemies into your hand." Deborah could say, "Up! for this is the day in which the Lord hath delivered Sisera into thine hand." But there were no words of rebuke for the men of Judah from the lips of

Samson. How could he rebuke them for their willingness to remain in bondage? was he not himself virtually in bondage to Philistines? — but bound by his passions, unable to deliver himself from Philistine women. Neither could he stand before them like Gideon and say, "As I do, so shall ye do." For his was an unworthy example to the people of God.

There were those of Judah in other days who did not live up to the dignity of which Jacob spoke: "Judah is a lion's whelp ... the sceptre shall not depart from Judah" (Genesis 49:8-12). In the days of Joash we read, "After the death of Jehoiada the priest, came the princes of Judah to the king ... and they forsook the house of the Lord ... and served idols, and wrath came upon Judah and Jerusalem" (2 Chron. 24:17, 18). Again on another occasion in Israel's history we read, "The nobles of Judah put not their hand to the work of the Lord."

Like Joseph's brethren in earliest days they were willing to hand over their own flesh and blood to their enemies. "And Judah said, What shall it profit us if we slay our brother and conceal his blood? Let us sell him" (Genesis 37:26). Thus the men of Judah said, "We will bind thee fast and deliver thee unto the hands of the Philistines, but surely we will not kill thee." Their hands would not be stained with his blood, but they would deliver him to those who were seeking to destroy him. Are we not reminded of the words of the Saviour: "He that delivered me unto thee hath the greater sin" (John 19:11)?

And when he came unto Lehi, the Philistines shouted against him, and amazingly we read, "The Spirit of the Lord came mightily upon him, and the cords that were upon his arms became as flax that was burned with fire, and his bands loosed from off his hands"! God did not fail His failing servant. He always abideth faithful. So, unfaithful to his Nazarite vow, disobedient to the commandments of the Lord, yet the Spirit of the Lord was with him in mighty strength. With the jawbone of an ass he slew a thousand men. God's purpose was being worked out. Samson was destroying Philistines. God was finding occasion against them.

Amidst all the failure upon which it has been our sad portion to meditate, the closing verses of this chapter (15) seem to be the brightest. This is the last time we read of "the Spirit of God coming mightily upon him". In the next chapter (16) we read, "He wist not that the Lord had departed from him." Here he calls upon the Lord in his sore thirst, he acknowledges "this great deliverance", he takes the place of "thy servant", he recognises that Philistines are uncircumcised, the enemies of the Lord. He will here, at least, earn his place among the heroes of faith in Hebrews 11. "The time would fail me to tell of Gideon, Barak, Samson, Jephthah and David." It is also here that we read, "He judged Israel in the days of the Philistines twenty years."

The Lord did not abandon His servant when he was surrounded by the enemy, neither did He fail to answer him when he cried in his sore thirst. What a contrast is found in Psalm 22:4,5 between our blessed Lord and Samson and all other men. "Our fathers trusted in thee: they trusted, and thou didst deliver them. They cried unto thee, and were delivered: they trusted in thee, and were not confounded. But ..." He cried in the daytime and God answered not. What a glorious contrast! All for us men and our salvation.

It should be noted that it is at this particular time that

God intervened and "clave an hollow place that was in the jaw, and there came water thereout; and when he had drunk, his spirit came again and he revived: wherefore he called the name 'Enhakkore'" — the well of him that called. Surely this poor man cried and the Lord heard him. An experience blessedly common amongst those who trust a faithful God.

However long the good period lasted at the end of chapter 15, Samson still shows a liking for Philistine women. First a harlot (16:1-3) and then Delilah (v. 4). How the words of James fall with power upon our ears: "Ye adulterers and adulteresses, know ye not that the friendship of the world is enmity with God? whosoever therefore will be a friend of the world is the enemy of God." One marvels at the way in which, totally infatuated by Delilah, he seems to completely trust her and confide in her, even while on a series of occasions it must have been evident to him that she was plotting with his enemies to bring him into captivity. He put his head in her lap when she had men lying in wait to overcome him, reminding us that "the whole world lieth in the lap of the wicked one" — nursed to sleep, feeling the warmth of the world's lap, lulled to slumber on the brink of doom.

How foolish he was! so strong, yet no match for the wiles of Delilah. Even as we, though "not ignorant of his devices", are no match for the wiles of the devil. He is not only a roaring lion seeking whom he may devour, but "that old serpent, the devil" — the deceiver, the beguiler. He is still the same; and could not Paul write, "I fear, lest by any means, as the serpent beguiled Eve through his subtilty, so your minds should be corrupted from the simplicity that is in Christ" (2 Cor 11:3)?

How the adversary used the tears of a woman to beguile and ensnare a strong man! Had it been a matter of bravery or warfare, he would have fought and been triumphant, but he could be worn down by the tears of the women that he loved. Does not Peter come to one's mind? strong, brave man that he was, and no doubt sincere when he avowed that he would die for his Lord, yet in the presence of a maid he could deny the Saviour, saying, "I know Him not."

Notice the tears and the pleas of these Philistines: "Samson's wife wept before him the seven days while the feast lasted, and it came to pass on the seventh day, that he told her, because she lay sore upon him" (14:17). Again when he loved Delilah: "Behold, thou hast mocked me and told me lies: now tell me, I pray thee" (16:10). "How canst thou say, I love thee, when thine heart is not with me? thou hast mocked me these three times" (16:15). "And it came to pass, when she pressed him daily with her words, and urged him, so that his soul was vexed unto death, he told her all his heart" (16:16,17).

What warnings lie here for all who love the Lord and would seek to please Him. One of the most difficult issues in life is to resist the pull of affection. In this as in every other circumstance our blessed Lord is the perfect example. See Mark 3:31: "There came then his brethren and his mother, and, standing without, sent unto him, calling him. And the multitude sat about him, and they said unto him, Behold, thy mother and thy brethren without seek for thee." But He to whom the will of God was always of paramount importance said, "Whosoever shall do the will of God, the same is my brother, and my sister, and mother." Did He not lay before His hearers the demands of true discipleship? "Except a man hate his father, and mother, and wife, and children, and brethren, and sisters, yea, and his own life also, he cannot be my disciple."

However, Samson and Delilah are a picture of a born-again man loving an unsaved woman, and her affection being used by the adversary to loving him into bondage. This incident is therefore a warning to any young man or woman who is considering an unequal yoke in marriage. My dear young friend, link with a worldling and you will find that such a partner, though so charming, considerate and loving, will have no interest in spiritual things, will not want you to become something for God. Such a partner will bring you down, will rob you of the time you know you ought to spend in prayer and meditation on His word. He or she will want the place in your heart and life that only Christ should have. Her tears, her voice, will doubtless be used in a variety of ways — hear the word of God in the beginning: "because thou hast hearkened unto the voice of thy wife ..." and many a saint of God has followed the same path since. Please do not be so foolish as to think that you will be the exception to the general rule, that you will be able to lead that unconverted partner to Christ. Hundreds have tried it before you and miserably failed. Take warning, lest what happened to Samson happens to you. Was he not eventually "wretched, and miserable, and poor, and blind, and naked"?

The wiles of Delilah succeeded in bringing down this strong man as he said, "If I be shaven, then my strength will go from me, and I shall become weak, and be like any other man" (16:17). Just the same today. Strong, young men for God if beguiled by the world into paths of disobedience lose their strength, their liberty to serve God, their spiritual discernment: the light that is in them becomes darkness — beware!

In passing let us notice that the Philistines would pay well to bring Samson down. How much Delilah would benefit by her treachery! Were there not five lords of the Philistines, and each was willing to pay her eleven hundred pieces of silver, making a total of five thousand five hundred pieces of silver. The devil was prepared to pay a large price to bring this strong man into bondage. He still has his ministers, transforming themselves into ministers of righteousness, determined to do the same thing: to cause the fall of anyone who could be used mightily for God. Did not the Saviour say in His day of another, "Woe unto that man by whom the Son of Man is betrayed"?

What a sad picture Samson presents in the closing days of his life. The Philistines took him, put out his eyes, brought him DOWN to Gaza, bound him with fetters of brass, and he did grind in the prison house. They said, as they gathered together to offer a great sacrifice unto Dagon, their god, "Our god hath delivered Samson our enemy into our hand" (16:24). They called him "our enemy, the destroyer of our country, which slew many of us." In spite of so much failure he had accomplished much for God, and had the enemy in constant fear. We can only add, "Would that their tribute had been far more true of him!"

What a lovely word, however, is this: "Howbeit the hair of his head began to grow again after he was shaven." Amid the sufferings of his prison experience, though bound and blind, the features of the Nazariteship were beginning to show again. Doubtless sorrow, remorse, contrition had produced repentance, not only now the external features, but the inward moral condition — Nazariteship of heart.

My brother, have you failed, sinned, let the Lord down? There is room for recovery! The hair of your head can grow again — repentance and recovery can be yours.

Truly a triumphant though tragic end was Samson's. "The dead which he slew at his death were more than they which he slew in his life." Upon the roof of the house were three thousand men and women. Was that the whole number? what kind of house was this? were there any more under the roof, round about, who would be crushed by the collapse of the building? What an occasion God had found against the Philistines through this man whom God had said would begin to deliver Israel.

May I draw your attention to the closing scenes. At the end of a life that commenced in a home where the parents *looked up*, that proceeded with a constant *going down*, he eventually is *taken up* — "His brethren and all the house of his father came down, and took him, and brought him up, and buried him in the burying-place of Manoah his father." A life of so many mistakes, so many wanderings, so many strange loves, but in the end brought up to the burying-place of Manoah his father. Can I see a picture here that would comfort the hearts of the saints. As we look back (as I look back) over a life lived for God, with all His faithfulness and all our unfaithfulness — so much going down instead of looking up — is it not a comfort to know that just as salvation is all of grace, so glorification is all of grace? The Lord is soon coming down to take us up to His Father's house:

"I will come again and receive you unto myself." What a glorious ending! What wondrous grace! And no doubt about the end: "God hath not appointed us to wrath, but to obtain salvation by our Lord Jesus Christ, who died for us, that, whether we wake (watch) or sleep (watch not) we should live together with Him" (1 Thessalonians 5:9-10).